HI WORLD, I'M DAD

of related interest

Raising a Whole Child
A family guide to supporting autistic children into adulthood
Carrie Cariello
ISBN 978 1 80501 111 8
eISBN 978 1 80501 112 5

I Will Die On This Hill
Autistic Adults, Autism Parents, and the
Children Who Deserve a Better World
Meghan Ashburn and Jules Edwards
Illustrated by Nathan McConnell
Foreword by Morénike Giwa Onaiwu
ISBN 978 1 83997 168 6
eISBN 978 1 83997 169 3

The Strengths-Based Guide to Supporting Autistic Children
A Positive Psychology Approach to Parenting
Claire O'Neill
ISBN 978 1 83997 215 7
eISBN 978 1 83997 216 4

What I Want to Talk About
How Autistic Special Interests Shape a Life
Pete Wharmby
ISBN 978 1 78775 827 8
eISBN 978 1 78775 828 5

Hi World, I'm Dad

How Fathers Can Journey to Autism Awareness, Acceptance, and Appreciation

James Guttman

Jessica Kingsley Publishers
London and Philadelphia

First published in Great Britain in 2025 by Jessica Kingsley Publishers
An imprint of John Murray Press

1

Copyright © James Guttman 2025

The right of James Guttman to be identified as the Author of the Work has been asserted by him in accordance with the Copyright, Designs and Patents Act 1988.

All rights reserved. No part of this publication may be reproduced, stored in a retrieval system, or transmitted, in any form or by any means without the prior written permission of the publisher, nor be otherwise circulated in any form of binding or cover other than that in which it is published and without a similar condition being imposed on the subsequent purchaser.

A CIP catalogue record for this title is available from the British Library and the Library of Congress.

ISBN 978 1 80501 424 9
eISBN 978 1 80501 425 6

Printed and bound in the United States by Integrated Books International

Jessica Kingsley Publishers' policy is to use papers that are natural, renewable and recyclable products and made from wood grown in sustainable forests. The logging and manufacturing processes are expected to conform to the environmental regulations of the country of origin.

Jessica Kingsley Publishers
Carmelite House
50 Victoria Embankment
London EC4Y 0DZ

www.jkp.com

John Murray Press
Part of Hodder & Stoughton Ltd
An Hachette Company

The authorised representative in the EEA is Hachette Ireland, 8 Castlecourt Centre, Dublin 15, D15 XTP3, Ireland (email: info@hbgi.ie)

Contents

Introduction —9

1: Getting Things Straight About Non-Verbal Autism —15
When Sounds Speak Louder than Words

2: Fear Itself —21
Overcoming Preconceptions in Parenting My Non-Verbal Son

3: If You're Something and You Know It —29
Father in a Strange Land

4: Musical Stares —35
Dealing with the Circle of Judgment from Strangers

5: Baby Bumps —43
Expecting the Unexpected

6: Every Kid Loves Birthdays...Right? —49
Adjusting Expectations

7: Welcome to the Undefined Worry —57
  The Stamina Required for Autism Parenting

8: Observing, Evolving, Understanding —67
  Learning New Strategies

9: Building Bridges of Understanding —73
  Teaching Trust through Everyday Moments

10: Rage, Restraint, and Raising a Non-Verbal Son —79
  Navigating Masculinity in SEN Parenting

11: Hello? Anyone There? —87
  The Struggle to Find Support as a Special Needs Dad

12: Make Room for Daddy —95
  Confronting Professional Bias and Embracing My Role as a Hands-On Dad

13: Entering His World, Redefining Mine —101
  The Journey to Acceptance and True Connection with My Son

14: Everything Can Change in a Moment... —105
  Refocusing on What Truly Matters as a Father

15: And a Child Shall Lead Them —115
  Finding Common Ground and Redefining My Role as a Father

16: Sorry My Kid's Trying to Eat Your Lunch —121
  Food, Eating, and Impulse Control

17: Calm Amid the Chaos —131
  Dealing with Sensory Overload

18: Her Brother, Not Her Burden —137
  Supporting Supportive Siblings

19: Feeling Alone While You're Surrounded —147
  Finding Your Tribe

20: Autism Awareness —157
  For a Family and for Society

21: Autism Acceptance —163
  For a Family and for Society

22: Autism Appreciation —169
  For a Family and for Society

23: Disability vs. this Ability —179
  It's All in the Perspective

24: Right Back to the Beginning —189
  Rethinking What You Assume Fatherhood Would Be

  Conclusion —199

Introduction

I'm a single dad to two brilliant kids. Lucas is my youngest, and this book is about him, and about how much I enjoy being his dad.

My son, along with his sister Olivia, is a dominant motivator for me. I want to be the best I can for them both. Each one of my children has a relationship with me that is so strong, yet so distinct from one another.

Lucas is unlike anyone I've ever known. He has a purity about him, a kind and loving nature that radiates in everything he does. There's a calm strength in the way he moves through the world, unaffected by the chaos that often engulfs us. His spirit is gentle but unwavering, and his presence in my life has been nothing short of transformative. He's changed how I see the world.

Every day, I'm inspired by Lucas to be a better version of myself. He has this incredible ability to bring out the best in me, simply by being who he is. He doesn't demand anything, yet he gives so much. His quiet resilience and boundless capacity for love are a constant reminder of what truly matters.

The bond we share is something I've never experienced before. It's deep and unspoken, rooted in a mutual understanding that goes beyond words. Lucas has taught me more about life, love, and what it means to be human than anyone else ever could.

If I said all this as a mom, the reaction from others would be more muted than I get as a dad. The positive outlook I have on Lucas may be unique, but the fatherly angle presents a different spin for many. To be honest, I don't entirely get it.

When I get going with one of my flowery expressions of love for Lucas, I'm usually met with a congratulatory speech about how "most dads" aren't like me. It's followed up by a horror story about some fair-weather father who ran off or who does nothing to help with his child's care. The bar is so low on fathers that many just simply need to show up to get their participation trophy. They refer to watching their own children as "babysitting." That's insane.

In theory, people who hear about my involvement say they love it. Mars may need moms, but Earth needs dads. No one expects the words I write to come from a man. Seriously. I write a blog that literally has the words "I'm Dad" in the title. Still people leave comments about what a wonderful mother I am.

Good mama 🤍 🙏

In a world that cries out for male role models, you'd think a father so involved in the life of his special needs son would be something that most people would applaud, right?

Well, they do...when I'm writing. Yet for some in the system and community, I'm still expected to go sit in the corner with the other dudes when the parenting time truly begins. Basically, they say they want dads to do more. Yet when the fathers take the reins and play a proactive role in the daily needs of their children, especially special needs children, everyone gets weird.

One of my earliest and weirdest interactions was with Lucas's preschool coordinator when he made his transition to kindergarten. We were setting up his program for the following year and the meeting would be by phone.

I called in and a woman (the preschool coordinator) answered. When she did, she was floored by the fact that I—the dad—was the one calling in alone.

"Are we just waiting for Lucas's mom?"

"No, I'm sorry. She isn't able to call in today."

She then let out this nervous laugh, like Cinderella's Godmother sitting on a porcupine, and said, I kid you not:

"Oh! Oh. Ha ha! Okay. That's good. We like fathers here, too! Ha ha ha!"

"Um... Good? That would be weird if you didn't."

Why wouldn't I be involved? These are my children. They're half me. I don't see it any other way. They are my legacy and represent my name to the world. I have felt connected to my role in their lives since they first showed up. I remember those days as if they happened yesterday.

In this book I want to challenge the traditional notions of fatherhood, especially in the context of raising a child with special needs. My journey with Lucas has shown me that being a father means stepping into roles that society often reserves for mothers, and doing so with pride and purpose. It's not strange or unusual; it's simply what parenting should be.

I want to shed light on the many beautiful realities of having a non-verbal son with autism, a perspective I call "autism appreciation." This concept is at the heart of everything I write. Lucas is who he is, with all his unique and wonderful traits, *because of autism*, not despite it.

I also want to share the journey that took me there. This didn't happen overnight, and the world Lucas opened up for me took time and patience on both our parts. I want to share that with you and anyone else who will listen. My son is the greatest boy in the world to me, and I wouldn't trade him for anything. I want everyone to know that.

INTRODUCTION

Through these pages, I aim to share the profound lessons Lucas has taught me, and to celebrate the incredible bond we share—one that defies conventional expectations and redefines what it means to be a parent.

CHAPTER 1

Getting Things Straight About Non-Verbal Autism

When Sounds Speak Louder than Words

Non-verbal autism doesn't mean silent.

Sorry for that abrupt start. I wanted to make sure that if someone picks up this book and decides to not read another word, at least they would get that key piece of information. It's one of two things I know for sure, but I never would have guessed before having a non-verbal son with autism.

Non-verbal is a misnomer for those who aren't defining "verbal" correctly. It refers to spoken word but, at least in the case of my son, it doesn't mean "mute." For him, non-verbal means the absence of verbal language. When it comes to other sounds, this kid does vocal gymnastics on the same level as the guy from the *Police Academy* movies.

Lucas, at present, is a teenage boy, and he is the loudest person you'll ever meet despite never speaking a word in his life. The sounds that come out of his mouth aren't there for communication; they are expressions of joy, anguish, and whatever deep emotions he wishes to express. Often, they seem to come flying out with passion unlike I've ever witnessed.

When you realize that his sounds are the product of his feelings, it makes sense that they are booming and persistent. My son feels things deeper than anyone else I've ever known. Positive or negative, his emotions burn brighter than mine by a mile, and that's saying a lot. I get all up in my feelings, as the kids say.

Lucas gets all up in his feelings too. But he not only gets up in them; he wraps them around himself, downs three Red Bulls, and bounces off the walls like he's on an all-encompassing trampoline. Simply put, my boy lives the hell out of life. He's a rock star without groupies, parties, drugs, and, uh, rock music. Sorry. That analogy sounded better at the start of the sentence. You get the idea, though.

With screams emanating from his room at all hours of the night, I've often joked that he could be having coke parties in there and we'd never know. If I ever swung the door open to find him doing a conga line with the New York Jets cheerleaders, I would, of course, be surprised...but not *too* surprised. Anything can happen with him, and the noise coming out of his room is an expression of excitement unlike anything I've ever heard before.

These sounds, however, are jarring when taken out of context. A few years ago, I woke up in the middle of the night to blood-curdling screams from down the hall. My first instinct, in my half-asleep state, was that it was my neurotypical daughter being bludgeoned in her room. Imagine waking up in a horror movie. That's what happened. I nearly fell out of bed as I rushed to the hallway, ready to fight whoever was in my house.

Then I realized it was Lucas. I paused, got back into bed, and drifted back to sleep with his ear-piercing screeches still ringing out. This was a sound that, if from one kid, would jolt me awake in a panic. Same sound—other kid—I drift off to blissful slumber. It's like nothing to me at this point. I can sleep through it like it's a lullaby.

For those outside my home, these shrieky shouts are not the same thing. This invisible sound that follows us like a soundtrack can be surprising to some. Hearing him, even from afar, is strange, and most people try to assign it to some sort of context. It has led to some sitcom levels of misunderstanding.

This is best exemplified during a phone call I had with Cablevision, back when my son was still little. Barely five, Lucas was jumping for joy in the living room and showing his decibel-breaking excitement over a video on his iPad. I was down the hall, with the door closed, trying to fix an issue with our Cable service.

Lucas's yells were still barreling through my door much

louder than I realized. It's hard to escape them when you're in the same house and, having so much exposure to them, I hadn't even noticed.

The call had been somewhat frustrating. I wasn't happy with the length of our call, but the customer service guy was trying to keep me talking. They love to chat with you so that you don't suddenly yell out "Cancel!" That's what this guy did. Pleasantries peppered the technical discussion. As he was typing and waiting for a manager to assist him, he decided to make small talk by commenting on the shrieks he could hear in the background.

"No problem, Mr. Guttman, I will get right on that. Say, do you have birds?"

Ugh. I knew why he was asking, but wasn't in the mood to do an autism TED Talk for the Cable rep. It did strike me as funny that the shouts resembled birds, as I had never really thought about it until this point.

I would have commended him for this connection, but wasn't here for an educational seminar; I was here to fix my Cable box so I could watch television. Birds? Come on, dude. Who cares? Get me back *Showtime*.

"Birds? No. I don't have birds."

The rep continued on, explaining whatever it was he was explaining, The high-pitched shouts persisted in the distance. Amid the discussion about Cable packages and replacement equipment, this dude decided to stop and see if perhaps I had forgotten that I had a collection of exotic winged creatures flying loudly through my home.

I'm serious. He really asked again. I had already told him not a minute earlier.

"Hey...are you sure you don't have birds?"

Am I *sure I don't have birds?* What the hell? Does he think I have some sort of underground black market feather business? If I did, why would I confide in the Cable man?

No wonder there's a four-hour wait to speak to a person at Cablevision customer service. Okay, palooka, two strikes and you're out. You wanna play? We'll play.

"No. I told you that I don't have birds. That's my son. He has autism and he's screaming in the other room."

And we wait.

And wait.

And after what must have felt like an eternity to him, he responded.

"Oh."

"Yeah. *'Oh.'* Can we fix my Cable now, please?"

And that's how the Cable guy learned that non-verbal doesn't mean silent. Be grateful you found out in a book.

This isn't the only stunning revelation I've had about autism since my son came into our lives. People often forget that there was a time when I didn't have a special needs child. I endured the scare tactics and television cliches too. So many of the misunderstandings and false pieces of information were things that I needed to unlearn. It's been a process and, in that process, I've had to teach others.

CHAPTER 2

Fear Itself

Overcoming Preconceptions in Parenting My Non-Verbal Son

As Lucas's dad, I've experienced behaviors that I never imagined and become accustomed to so many norms that I never dreamed of. Having a son like mine has been eye-opening in all the best ways.

For those who think it has been difficult for us, I wouldn't necessarily disagree. Parenting in general is difficult, and each child has their own set of difficulties. I love my boy, though, and caring for him has been the most welcome difficulty I could ever want in my life.

My goal has always been to share this experience with the world. Few can genuinely appreciate the beauty of having a boy like mine. Lucas marches to the beat of his own drummer and that drummer plays a specialized tune that few, if any, others have danced to. I have never met someone like my son, whether that person is on the spectrum or not. There's only one Lucas, and I have him.

The reason everyone isn't raving about the beauty that comes with having a non-verbal child like mine is because most people don't know these things about him. They only see my son when he's causing an issue. Think about it. Who's looking at Lucas and me in a supermarket as we quietly stroll down the bread aisle?

I mean, aside from those checking us out because we're so fetching, no one pays attention to what we're doing until he's doing something that breaks the silence. The happy moments are left unnoticed. His sweet expressions of love and kindness are overlooked.

It's when he's screaming in the cereal aisle that they look up. They see his meltdowns or distracting reactions. From 10 feet away, they'll try to sneak a glance at why he's whining and quickly look away before being spotted.

Witnessing me try to calm him down becomes the only point of view they have of my son—and with him, every person with needs like his. In that moment, we unwittingly represent an entire community. The only thing some of these strangers may know about autism is from a far-off view of my son and our family.

And they think, "Oh wow. It's sad. That must be so hard for his dad."

The short answer to that? Yes. During times that my son is overwhelmed or doesn't understand what's happening, it's sad and heartbreaking and all the things people tend to imagine in their worst-case scenarios.

Of course, the same can be said for parenting any child, on or off the spectrum. That's a raising-kids-thing, it's not autism-specific. I have a teenage daughter who is not on the spectrum. Non-verbal kids don't have the market cornered on heart-breaking; they just have their own set of things that cause it.

Lucas may struggle with life skills or caring for himself. That's heartbreaking. Lucas will also never get stood up for the prom or fail to get into a school he was eager about. There's a balance of great things he will miss out on and terrible moments he will never experience.

I know the common response to me projecting thoughts onto strangers seeing us from afar. It sounds like I'm being paranoid by guessing the thoughts of others; I'm not. What I'm saying is true and I know it is. Yet well-meaning friends will try to talk me out of that train of thought. They look me in the eye with all the compassion they can muster and, as they place a sympathetic hand on my shoulder, they'll assure me that "No one is really thinking that your life must be sad because you have to care for a kid like Lucas."

Oh, but they do. I know they do. How? Because, as I mentioned earlier, there was a time before I ever knew a person with non-verbal autism. During that time, I would have thought like that.

Keep in mind, I'm not pointing out this train of thought as if it's some sort of mean-spirited thing being done by those in the distance. For the most part, there's no ill intent from the silent starers. Sure, some might get all holier than thou in their minds, but those people would get that way with any situation they spy from afar. Most observers come at it from a place of compassion. They assign pity to what they believe to be a terrible situation.

I get it. It's not true, but I get it. That's why I take the time to explain the reality to those who ask. I write about the reality for those to read. I set an example for those who are peering from behind the produce.

So let's just lay it all on the table. My son has what some call "severe autism" or "low-functioning autism." The terms are jarring to hear and harder to say. During his roughest meltdowns, the visual is shocking for some. I get that and don't fault anyone for feeling the way they do.

The truth is that those moments are fewer and farther in between than many would realize. Even when Lucas and I encounter those tough moments, they're not as emotionally devastating as they appear to be.

When he was younger, they took more of a toll on us. More frequent and impactful, our misunderstandings were still new, and handling them was still a work in progress. Today, those times are anticipated, and dealing with them can feel almost routine. That's why they don't happen as much.

While I have this firsthand experience, you have to remember that there were over 30 years when I hadn't. I lived a full life before Lucas's birth, and I lived in a world around people without children like mine. I experienced them when they weren't always at their most tolerant behavior in the middle of a crowded shopping mall. I know what people think and the fears they hold in their hearts over finding themselves in a situation like mine.

Before Lucas, the thought of having a special needs child sent shivers down my spine. It was the worst-case scenario and I dreaded the possibility. Delays and disabilities were the Keyser Söze of parenting. Breastfeed; don't breastfeed. Vaccinate; don't vaccinate. Play classical music; don't play classical music. There were so many warnings to watch out for or else "the autism will get you." I felt fear for those who had kids like that, and I worried about my own personal future when I saw them. You don't get much more honest than that. It's exactly how I felt.

There's a reason that you don't often hear special needs parents admit that. Recalling that time in my life is hard because I know now how wrong I was. I didn't have a child with pronounced delays who I loved; I just had the image of someone else's kid. I didn't love their kid and that made it scary. That's why I felt the way I did back then, but it's still difficult to put on paper.

Had I not chosen to write about my son in order to show others our world, I don't know if I would have ever admitted it. The guy I was when I thought that way feels like a guy I knew in another lifetime.

While it makes me sick to say it out loud, it's important to acknowledge it. So often, parents like me are ready to be offended. They pretend like they always knew how strong their bond would be with a child that hadn't yet arrived, and couldn't care less if they were born with special needs. Me? Nah. I was scared. I didn't know Lucas yet. I didn't want to have a child with what the world calls "disabilities."

That's how I know there are people out there with that same viewpoint. I also know that it's a perspective built on ignorance and lack of exposure to the very thing they fear. These people judging from afar don't want Lucas because they don't know Lucas. If they knew him like I did, they'd be trying to come hang out at my house and watch Raffi videos. Then, when we weren't looking, they'd try to steal him away and take him back to their own house.

Luckily, my boy is a gigantic squishmellow of a person and pretty hard to nab. I call him the Round Mound of Sound—a name I stole from an obscure wrestling manager from the '70s. All the better to wrap my arms around during my lowest moments. If I ever feel down, I run to him, and he rarely pushes me away. Even as a teenager, he still lets me hug him. I attribute that to autism, and it's part of the benefits that come with having him as my kid.

Lucas makes me happy, lifting me up during my darkest times. Alongside his neurotypical older sister, he's my reason to get up every morning, push on in my life, and try to be a better person.

He keeps me sober. He keeps me out of jail. He keeps me alive. And he doesn't even know it.

Being the father to a special needs child gives me pride and honor. I get to have a relationship that few people ever get to experience. The way that he and I interact is unique and special. I may sound like a broken record, but that's fine. I love the song it plays. I love him with all my heart. I'll repeat it forever.

CHAPTER 3

If You're Something and You Know It

Father in a Strange Land

To this day, I associate Music Together class with my son's autism diagnosis. I'm not sure how long we went for, but it felt like 150 years. Each week was more surprising than the last, and this agonizing Saturday tradition became about autism awareness, self-awareness, and coming to grips with a lot.

My trepidation in taking Lucas to a Music Together class predated any diagnosis. In fact, he was barely showing signs when I began. Sadly, this simmering apprehension involved the mere fact that I was a father going to a "Mommy and Me" class alone.

I knew the way fathers handling activities traditionally seen as "mom" things were viewed by many in society. People get weird with that stuff.

I know this because when my daughter, Olivia, was a baby, I took her to a make-up class by myself once.

Olivia's mom handled her music classes mostly on her own, which is why I became the one to take Lucas years later. But I offered to take Olivia one weekday morning to a make-up class a few towns over. It would be a different teacher in a different location. I had met her regular one. This one was a stranger...and boy was she strange.

From the start, I knew something was off about this teacher. I could tell she wasn't just antisocial by giving me the cold shoulder because I could see the way her face lit up when talking to the other mothers. It spoke volumes.

The common feeling of passive judgment swept over me. It's the same feeling you get when you can tell a person is put off by your color, race, or last name. I was familiar with that tense atmosphere that always took a few minutes to pinpoint. Someone was thinking something about you, but not saying it. This was that feeling.

I'm going to call this teacher Sandra, not to protect her identity, but because I don't remember her name. This was over a decade ago and she was awful. I've already rewritten over that file in my mental hard drive.

Sandra started off slow but deliberate in what I felt was her disgust for me. As we played with bells and scarves, she would walk around the circle singing, and always had to correct my movements by adjusting my arm as if we were at an Orangetheory fitness class. If I was ringing the bell in tune with the music, she'd find something wrong with how I was doing it. No words were spoken. It was just a silent hand-over-hand to set me straight. I felt like a second grader being corrected when tying his shoes. I didn't like it, but chalked it up to another annoying aspect of parenthood.

It all led to an exchange that forever damaged the song "Happy and You Know It" for me.

The song is common for every kid. Even if you're not happy, you know it. It's the song we all learn at the age of two and become experts in by the age of three. That was the game. If you're happy and you know it, do a thing. Whatever. Do something physical. You're happy.

It was time to belt out the childhood classic and I already knew it by heart. With Olivia in my lap, I began singing along. All was going well until Sandra told us to tap our heads. So I tapped my daughter's head. Everyone was singing. Everyone was smiling. Then the singing stopped. Sandra stopped singing.

"No. Not like that. Use her hands to tap her head."

Of course she was barking orders at me and only me across a staring circle of women. The instrumental music on CD was still playing over us so I could barely understand what she was saying. I caught "tap her head," so when the singing continued, I did that again. Tap, tap, tap.

At this point, she became very annoyed and shut the music

abruptly. All the moms and babies froze and watched as this demon with a tambourine shuffled out on her knees and came right up to me to scold me.

"No! Not **your** hand! **Her** hands! You have to use **her** hands!"

This wasn't done in a tone you'd expect from a music teacher for toddlers; it was the inflection you'd hear when a plane's going down and they're trying to get you to press the right button. Only this wasn't an airplane. We were sitting crisscross applesauce in socks with babies in our laps.

Sandra then showed me what she meant by taking my daughter's hands and doing this incredibly difficult task for me. I guess she thought I needed the visual. At that point, she shuffled back to her spot and continued the song. Each time she changed the movement, she'd glare at me and exaggeratedly nod her head when I did it correctly. Outside of the singing, the rest of the room had grown rather quiet. I wasn't sure if it was out of pity for me or fear of becoming her next target.

You know what's weird? I tell that story and people act like there was something I should have done. They tell me all the reactions they would have had, especially Long Island dads. They turn Music Class into a Battle Royal and believe that freaking out is somehow realistic. It's not like I could headbutt her. This is real life.

There seemed to be an underlying issue that I wasn't privy to here, and I feel like challenging the teacher's authority over the toddler circle would have just ruined the class for everyone. I was here for my daughter. I hadn't even been a father for a year.

People say I should have left. How? I was tasked with bringing my daughter to a single solitary music class—something she loved—but I had to leave early because the teacher was being all mean to me?

"Well, James, what did she do?"

"She made me let Olivia tap her own head!"

What could I really do? A voice in my brain gave me many options and all of them were insane. I try to drown that voice out when I can. Instead, I absorbed the rest of this awkward class and took my kid back home.

If you're wondering if I am embellishing this story or taking it harder than I should, there is actual proof to the contrary. After returning from her next scheduled class, my then-wife told me that one of the other moms from our class was at the same make-up class that I was. She told me this woman said, "I felt so sorry for your husband at that make-up class. None of us knew what was going on. She was really mean to him."

Yep. If you're a judgmental jerk who pushes parents away from helping their kids depending on their gender, tap your head. No. Not like that. You're doing it wrong.

One would think that an experience like this would scare me away from wood blocks and triangles, but it didn't. I was the go-to parent for Lucas's music time. This was my time to shine. We'd show the Sandras of the world. We'd show 'em all.

Little did I know that those fateful Saturday mornings would go on to become a pivotal moment in our lives. We learned nothing about pitch and harmony. We learned everything about autism awareness.

CHAPTER 4

Musical Stares

Dealing with the Circle of Judgment from Strangers

P arents with a baby first showing early signs of delay know the feeling of a million eyes silently judging. In our case, it was about 60 eyes. Maybe 59 if one of the other parents in the class had a glass eye or something. There has to be a margin of error on that. Either way, people were looking.

Lucas wasn't just under a microscope; he was under a lollipop drum and a nursery rhyme CD that cost $75. He was definitely a focal point for many there. The way my kid stood out wasn't simply by non-participation either. I had been in that situation before. This wasn't that.

Years earlier, his big sister had gone to a TOTnastics gym class where she refused to speak to the teacher. It was so weird. I guess it was shyness, but she'd just sit there during song time and stare.

No one really cared. The few times I apologized to Mr. Charles, he said it was fine and kids do it. So, yeah, I was aware of the quiet game. If Lucas just did that, we'd have nothing to talk about here. However, if you think that's the case, you don't know my kid.

The fact that I was the only solo father routinely taking his son to these classes—a major point just years earlier with my daughter that fateful day—was a complete non-issue.

I say that, but I don't know if it was an issue for others around us. People may have been watching and murmuring about my gender. I just didn't notice because of everything else going on. It would be like worrying if your shoes are tied as you go down on the Titanic.

Whatever they were doing or thinking was their business, I was laser-focused on Lucas. I was always watching him to make sure he was safe and not doing something monumentally inappropriate. I tuned out the world as I scanned his behavior for all the "red flags" that I already knew were there. In this class, however, I didn't have to scan too deeply. Music Together was his stage; warning signs were his performance. This was Lucas's coming-out party.

Of course, the little things I saw at home were there. When the teacher came around, hunched over, to hand us a bell or a scarf, he never took one. She'd dangle these colorful pieces of translucent ribbon before his eyes and he'd look right through them. No attempts were made to grab at them. Excitement rarely showed in his face, and never for something musical. Babies a fraction his age reached for these toys with more vigor than my son did. He couldn't care less.

My kid didn't sing or hum. He didn't want to strum the guitar or tap the drums. When she handed out those stupid eggs with beads inside, he tried to eat them. I felt like she could have paraded an elephant into the room and he'd fall asleep.

Out of all her gimmicks, the only thing my son liked were the blue sticks with ridges all along the side. We were supposed to drum the floor with them or rub them together. Lucas wasn't much for the whole make-fire routine, but he loved hitting them against the ground. It was one of the only things he really did in that class.

Seeing this caused so much excitement that I ran to Amazon and grabbed a 20-pack of them. Why so many? I don't know. Maybe we wanted to use them more than once. Badaboom ching. Leave me alone. I was excited.

Once those sticks arrived at home, I pulled them out and placed them in his hand.

And he didn't care.

They might as well have been scarves. From that day forward, they lived in a clear storage box in our bookshelf until they were discarded somewhere. Swing and a miss.

With no instruments to grab his attention and no verbal language for him to sing the songs, one would think that

Lucas did nothing in this class. But oh, one would be wrong. As I mentioned earlier, it was showtime, folks. My little stinger had a few things on his agenda with one specific item atop that checklist. He was determined to make it happen.

His main mission was to place his face on the cold classroom floor.

Does it sound like I'm being sarcastic or overdoing it for effect? I'm not. When I say this was his mission, I mean it. All Lucas wanted was to push the side of his cheek against the dusty and dirty tiles we had all been walking on. Remember those tiles in your elementary school? The ones that would instantly turn your jeans gray if you dared to kneel on them? Yeah. These were those tiles. The first time he tried to do it, I nervously laughed it off.

"What are you doing, buddy? No floor. Ha ha."

People looked over and smiled. It was cute, I guess. A little silly, but cute.

I lifted him up...and he went right back down. I'd cradle his head a few inches from the ground and he'd push down with even more force. Soon, I was dribbling his head like a slow-motion basketball against the tile. Everyone was watching, but that didn't stop him. He just kept going. He always kept going.

That's the thing. Lucas didn't care what these people thought. He still doesn't, and while I've come to appreciate that part of his personality, I hadn't yet. A simple "cut the crap" never landed, and no matter how many times I stopped him, he just kept going back to the well.

I didn't know what the hell was happening. Other babies were singing "Up and Down with Captain Brown." My baby is turning his face into a magic eraser and eating maracas eggs.

Keep in mind, this was a hard floor. My ultimate fear was that he was going to push back against my cradled hands with such force that he ends up cracking his skull open. I pictured horrific scenes of splattered pieces of Lucas brain all over the screaming faces of parents and those stupid blue sticks. The scarves would run red with blood, and we'd almost definitely lose our musical privileges.

Those reading this right now might wonder why I didn't stop going when he showed he didn't care about it. I know I would wonder the same thing, and today, we would have absolutely tapped out after the first two weeks.

However, those who have experienced a period of hazy confusion like I had during these transformative years get it. I couldn't take him out of class for behavior like that. That would be like saying it out loud.

Saying what out loud?

Exactly.

Leaving would have felt like admitting something that I wasn't ready to acknowledge yet. All I thought was, what would I tell people? I left because my son wouldn't stop trying to put his face on the floor? I could picture their facial expressions already. I might as well scream "special needs" from the rooftop.

I already saw enough faces from the critic around me in the judgmental circle. People would glance over but not say anything. No one was rude or pushy, but you could tell when they were being nosey. Who knows. Maybe they were being rude. Like I said, I was so laser-focused on Mr. Floorshine over here that I noticed nothing else.

One mom I already had an aversion to because she looked like a girl I had known and disliked when I was younger struck up a conversation with me before class began one week. My boy was lunging for the door and I was trying to corral him. Her kid was sitting quietly in front of her.

"Has he started school yet?"

Finally, someone was making regular conversation with me. He had. At this point in the class, his nursery school had already begun. I was just pleased that someone was talking to me. Granted, I was holding my son's shirt collar as he was stretching away from me like a cartoon mouse being held by the tail. Still, this was good. I could be social. We belong here.

"Yeah. He did. Last month."

"Oh, that's great. Has he told you he likes it? Has he said he likes his teacher?"

MUSICAL STARES

I wanted to toss a tambourine at this woman's head. She had been sitting next to us for nearly a year. The phrasing of her question was purposeful, and her attempt to squeeze out information felt, in the least, hurtful.

I wanted to say, "You know damn well he doesn't talk, jackass."

Instead, I just shrugged and said, "Yeah. He likes school."

She had seen how horrific our Saturday mornings had been. She knew what she was trying to ask. She'd seen everything I had. Aside from ignoring instruments and the face-floor dribble game, Lucas also did the routine actions of acting out. When he was done doing the face thing, he spent the rest of the class running for the exit. When we finally made it through the traumatic hour, he would stage one last battle against putting his shoes back on amid a cramped room of well-behaved toddlers.

With all that, I still needed to keep him pinned to my side at all times or he would dash off without warning. The door kept swinging open. He was trying to run. We were next to a train station. It was a major concern.

Still, he may have been rambunctious, but things hadn't been too bizarre.

And then...there was "the incident."

CHAPTER 5

Baby Bumps

Expecting the Unexpected

Before I write this, I just want to remind everyone that none of my stories are made up or exaggerated. Nothing has been added for dramatic effect. The names may have been changed to protect the innocent or forgotten, but the scenes always played out as they're written.

We had been going to this class for a while and my little guy was a not-so-little guy at this point. It was easy to lose sight of that fact because he had remained much younger in his tastes and behavior. Still, you could tell visually. This wasn't a baby any more.

When a couple in the class decided to bring in their actual infant, it was a reminder of what genuine babies look like. Their newborn was adorable, and it reminded me of bringing Lucas to one of his sister's Music Classes shortly after he was born. So cute. So sweet. You know the deal.

While I didn't know their names, I was happy to see the family so happy. Everyone was "ooing" and "ahhing" at this little bundle of newborn joy. The nostalgia in my head had me smiling too, a rarity for these classes.

Keeping with that rare theme, even Lucas noticed the four of them smiling. He peered over and slowly crawled over to their spot in the circle. I froze with trepidation and pride. For the first time ever, my little man was showing an interest in other people.

This was it. This was his time to shine. I had never seen this social side of him outside of his immediate family, and even then it was a rare occurrence. My brain began celebrating this turned corner and crafting scenarios where he starts doing all the things we had been praying for. This is our Saturday Morning miracle. Maybe he'll start talking on the car ride home!

I watched with pride as he sat right next to the newborn, who was laying on the floor beside him, and peered into her mother's eyes. The parents around us were now saying "aww" for my son. That had never happened in this class. My boy was adorable and creating a Hallmark Moment for us all to witness. The mom, with a sweet motherly smile, looked back at my precious boy.

"Hello there," she said with a softness in her voice.

Lucas looked at her with the sweetest face you could ever imagine. Then he took both of his hands and placed them behind his head like he was doing the "Macarena"...

And laid down on her baby.

I am not making this up. I am not exaggerating. I am not taking poetic license. He laid down on her freaking baby. That's the headline. His arms cradled behind his head like a Peanuts character staring at the clouds, Lucas used this infant's torso as a neck pillow and stared up at her mom with a massive grin.

Everyone paused to digest what exactly was happening. You couldn't really react to it immediately because it was so out-of-left field that you feel like the universe's simulation had just gone haywire. It took a moment to sink into us individually around the circle. Soon, the game of shocked dominoes began.

The gasps came in abundance and I shuffled across the circle on my knees to scoop him up as quickly as possible. I think I apologized. I hope I apologized. I don't know what I did. It felt like a fever dream.

The baby was alright, I guess. No one sued me or called the house. That's a good sign. It was, honestly, the most bizarre day of his young life, and for me, definitely top five.

Driving home, I couldn't stop talking out loud to him about it.

"Buddy. You laid down on that baby. What the hell? Lucas, you can't lay down on babies! They're not for laying down on!"

And he'd giggle and look out the window.

"I'm not joking. Do you understand me? You don't understand me."

I didn't know if we should ever go back, but we did. We only had a handful of classes left, the session was paid for already, and now I knew I just had to keep him away from, well, everyone.

There was, however, a straw that broke the camel's back for us. It was the last class we ever went to and how we left two classes unattended. I hate this story.

A few weeks later, we had come in early and our teacher had just returned from her own maternity leave a few weeks earlier. She was doting over her newborn at home and I was just grateful she didn't bring her in because my large son would've definitely laid down on her kid too.

Before class began, we were always treated to some sort of instrument to strum. It changed week to week, but the kids would crawl over and pluck the strings. It was cute. Lucas never cared. I barely did too, if I'm being honest. These classes started to feel like a condition of my probation or something.

It was only us and another mom with her baby. She was already deep in conversation with the teacher when we got there and sat in the still-empty circle. They were talking about the love babies have for music. Our musical mentor then decided to share a personal anecdote about that very subject and her infant's love of rhythm.

"Oh yes. Babies know music. Last week, we were playing music and Ruby started tapping. Tap, tap, tap. Joe and I were like, 'Oh no! Why is she doing tapping?! Is that a stim!? Does she have autism!?' No, no. Ha ha. She was just tapping the floor in rhythm with the music. We were like, 'Phew.' Ha ha."

It felt like I had gotten kicked in the stomach.

Again, the whole you-should-have-left crowd kicks in here, and again, I have a counterargument.

How could I walk out of this class because she said something against autism? To do so would be to admit that I thought my kid has autism. Get it? You can't get offended if you're still trying to accept whether your child has it or not. It would be an admission I wasn't ready for in the most defensive way possible.

Even crazier, my mind thought that maybe by her talking about it in front of us, she probably doesn't think Lucas has any special needs. Right?

To be fair, my instinct was to pick him up, kick the mandolin, and run out the door. I'm not kidding either. Even without admitting to myself that Lucas might have autism or special needs, despite the overwhelming evidence, I knew that this woman could go to hell. I was done that day.

That was the last class we went to. Lucas and I endured our final hour. It was all the same. Cheek on the floor, run for the door, nevermore. We did nothing musically together.

At the end, I didn't even put on his shoes; I carried him to the car in his socks.

And I told him on the way home:

"No more, buddy. That was our last music class. That lady sucks. All done."

And we were. We had bigger things to focus on and more square pegs to jam into round holes.

CHAPTER 6

Every Kid Loves Birthdays...Right?

Adjusting Expectations

It's easy for me to say that I wasn't the one who wanted to throw Lucas his second birthday party and I knew it would be a bust from the start, but that's not true. While Lucas's mom did a lot of the planning, I went along without raising a single issue. This was all in the midst of our Music Together adventure. He was two. That's what you do at two.

We held it at some kid's gym out on Long Island. You know the place I'm talking about because, if you have ever had a kid, you've been there. You're picturing it now. That's it.

Everything was foam and rubber. There were ropes and balls and all sorts of balance things to make any kid jump for joy. Well, *most* kids jump for joy.

Lucas wasn't having it from the get-go, and my boy, just

starting to get his footing to embark on his run-from-everything career, didn't want to stay put from the moment we arrived. The littlest sprinter was raring to go.

Rather than sit in the waiting area, he darted up and down the hallway with excitement that I still see him display today. I remember half-heartedly joking that he would love to run around the gym when the party started. I didn't realize how prophetic my words would be.

Lucas was stoked like he was on coke to run around that cliche gym. By that, I mean that he was excited to dash from wall to wall, without a second thought to the activity being presented or what was in his way. Kids were lining up and being given numbers to do some sort of organized ball nonsense; meanwhile my little guy was running full speed towards the janitor's closet…and crying when we wouldn't let him in or when he slammed his head into it at 90 miles per hour.

Even the parachute, much like the one I had purchased for our home earlier that year, did nothing. Lucas was too enamored with everything around him to focus on a single toy. The coach/teacher/person tried to get everyone to coax him back to the group by chanting his name. They all did. It gave me that sinking feeling the second it started.

"Lucas! Lucas! Lucas!"

I knew he wasn't coming and, of course, Lucas didn't care. He wasn't paying attention to what they were doing and the repetition of his name was immaterial. This was the same kid who would ignore me when I walked into the room. Having randos call his name, something I was still unsure if he even knew, was nothing. That couldn't stop his pursuit of, um, whatever he was pursuing around the perimeter of his party.

I can't blame the staff for this. No one, especially back then, really knew how to handle a boy like him. While chanting his name might not get a reaction other than the visceral misery of his father, knowing he will never respond, that might not be the case in all cases. Another boy with autism might come running and his parent might be offended if the chanting never came. Even then, I understood well-meaning people meaning well, even if it was torture.

It's one of the reasons why parties like these had to happen. No one is to blame, and even events that fall flat need to be tried, at least initially. They weren't disasters in the traditional sense. Lucas wasn't miserable, and while it didn't hit in the way we hoped, it still generated some photos and memories. It also showed us that big parties weren't something he was necessarily on board with.

That's an important aspect of autism parenting and one that I sometimes need others to point out. In fact, a year or two ago, I was talking to my daughter about doing presents on Christmas Eve. I mentioned wanting to do it early so Lucas wouldn't fall asleep, even though it would seriously throw off dinner time.

"It's okay. Lucas doesn't care about that stuff. We can give it to him whenever."

And she was right. He doesn't.

Saying it out loud, though, stings a bit. You pause for a second and wonder if you're discounting his abilities or underestimating his awareness. In reality, you're doing neither. You're showing that you truly know your child. Saying he doesn't care about opening presents when it's true isn't insulting; it's an acknowledgment that you understand him better than most people. It's showing that he doesn't need to do things our way in order to be accepted into our family. We're not pretending.

It's only when you haven't accepted your child's overall personality that you see elements of it as something to feel guilty about. Lucas doesn't like opening presents. It's the truth. It doesn't discount him as a person or a member of our family to admit it. It's actually the opposite.

This party was an example of that and showed me that Lucas doesn't need to do all the things that kids his age might do. He just needs to be happy.

Sure, we can have parties, but they'd be more for family and friends than my son. He'll be grateful to eat the food and see people, but he doesn't need a clown and a mariachi band to celebrate his big day. He just needs us. We're the clowns. We're the band.

In fact, we've never fully been sure if Lucas understands the concept of a birthday. Even more specific, I don't know if he necessarily follows the concept of days themselves, and whether any are special. It's such a strange thing to admit and a stranger thing to explain.

EVERY KID LOVES BIRTHDAYS...RIGHT?

There's no scenario where I can tell my son that we're doing something "on Tuesday" and have him grasp what I'm saying. I could make the same claim about telling him we are going somewhere "tomorrow." He doesn't think like that, and even if he did, he's never given any indication that he cares about such things. Wild, right? That's something that most people never even think about.

Birthdays, while vital to so many, aren't as important to him. Giving him a special day that fits his lifestyle is more important than some grand gala with a velvet rope and VIPs.

Trust me, we've done the VIP thing. That second birthday party was loaded with casual friends and old daycare acquaintances. In fact, it wasn't my boy's indifference to the parachute dance that turned me off from doing these parties again; it was some of our party guests.

One family we barely knew came from the daycare days and you couldn't miss them if you were in earshot. This mom and son were ripped right from a Scorsese movie. She was the kind of mother that spoke Long Island loud and proud. She was always yelling at her twins and finishing her sentences off with "Hah?"

We were entering the closing moments of the great play gym when this woman was, of course, shouting at her son. I don't know what he was doing, but it was probably something awful. He wasn't an angel.

"Stop it, Jimmy! Stop it, right now! Be good, hah! This party is supposed to be for Lucas!"

Of course, the kid had the same social graces as his mom and yelled back—across the entire gym—something that made me want to dropkick him into the cargo nets.

"Lucas doesn't even talk!"

Nice, right? You're probably thinking how you'd react to that. Admit it. Before you read what he said, you judged my line about the cargo net dropkick. Now you're probably picturing punting that little mook across the street yourself. You get it. You know why I didn't? Because I had less than half a second to think before big momma screamed back at her little demon spawn. That turned this stinging moment into a one, two punch.

"Yeah?! Well then, why don't you teach him!?"

Great comeback, Mom. No wonder this kid sucks. My brain switched from aggression to exhaustion immediately. I hated these people. The voice in my head said "screw this." And that was the last time we paid for a party that our kid wouldn't like.

That talking thing was a huge issue back then, and Mrs. Long Island* Mom hit a major sore spot with that, big time. All we wanted was for Lucas to talk. We were fixated on it. Thanks for the birthday reminder.

When you have a non-verbal kid, that's the only agenda at first. You put everything on the back burner in favor of

---

* (pronounced Lawnguyland)

language. Experts would ask what we wanted to work on, and "talking" was all we could say. How could we focus on anything else? It was like asking someone to do the dishes as your kitchen burns down. Get him talking...please!

CHAPTER 7

Welcome to the Undefined Worry

The Stamina Required for Autism Parenting

It's why I was in such a haze when we first approached an autism-friendly preschool for him. I will never forget that week. Still dying for a first word, I had put all my hope into this institution. I felt like this school was the final step to admitting that my boy had more than delays; he had real issues that needed deeper assistance.

I had done mental gymnastics to minimize obstacles that were becoming too large to ignore. It's easy to tell yourself that your kid is just slightly behind when others his age are saying words that he isn't. Now those kids his age were telling me jokes and he still wasn't speaking. We're falling too far behind to catch up on a magical weekend.

That's an in-your-face reality that, as a parent, you need to deal with at some point. Even the most positive among us have to go through a low point. It would be great to pretend like I never did. I wish I could offer some sort of phony higher-thinking moments during these dark times, but I can't. I had fear and heartache constantly. It makes me a little sick to think about it again.

We'd get those brochures and scan the websites with pictures of joyous families. Parents flanked by their special needs kids looked so happy. They were at parks and playing with a ball. I couldn't wrap my head around it. How are they smiling? That was everything I was currently digging my heels in and praying against.

It's a feeling of sadness mixed with guilt on two fronts. You're forced to deal, almost exclusively, with the things your child doesn't do when they first get diagnosed with autism. That's how it gets addressed. Unfortunately, this is at a time when other moms and dads are getting to talk about all their children's wonderful achievements. For a concerned parent to a child who might be on the spectrum, doctors only want to hear about what they *aren't* doing. That hurts to rehash over and over, visit after visit. Yet you do it. Each conversation is a reminder of how much unknown is still ahead.

I blamed myself for, if nothing else, simply inviting him into what I could only assume would be a complicated life. I chose to bring him into this world and make him a part of our family. Now, because of me and my selfish need for a child, this sweet little boy has what I kept thinking was a painful road ahead of him.

Of course, this was very early on in his life. We hadn't even started on the road, and all my assumptions were simply that. There was no sign of what it could look like other than guesswork. While those thoughts didn't even come close to matching the wonderful life that he has today, those fears at the time were real. If you love your child, you feel those fears and worries. They are not something a parent should feel shame about, yet almost all of us do.

The second part of my guilt dealt with the fact that I felt that shame. It was my guilt over feeling guilty. I felt bad about how I felt bad because, deep down, I knew not to feel bad. Was that bad?

Sound confusing? Welcome to my world back then. It was like my brain was telling myself, "Feeling sorry for your son is wrong." But how could I not? Wouldn't it be weirder if I didn't? A doctor says, "Your kid has autism." And I say, "Okay. Cool. Is there an Outback Steakhouse around here? I'm starving."

All this was hitting me in the face as we prepared for the orientation at my son's special needs preschool. I didn't talk much and plugged myself into my Xbox all day. I dug an isolated hole in my brain and just sat there.

Walking into that building was difficult. This was the first step towards autism, in my mind. There would be no more pretending and shrugging at people waiting on high fives. I had danced around it and tried to avoid the topic, but now it was real. We're on the grid—the autism grid.

Lucas's mom and I entered the school cafeteria, which felt

1000 feet wide. All I could see was a sea of tables with tissue boxes from wall to wall. Seated at each were weeping moms and dazed dads blankly staring in silence. Aside from sniffles, coughs, and Kleenex pulls, there wasn't a sound.

We took a seat and soon another couple sat across from us. My mind was in a million places, but I couldn't help but stare at them. I felt my brain was playing tricks on me because I was sure I knew who these people were. Maybe we were connected through the universe? Is this a glitch in the matrix?

It took about 10 minutes to realize that the wife and I had worked together for two weeks ten years earlier. Trying to place her in my mental history became my main focus for the opening of this presentation. I didn't even remember her name, so I never said anything, but it was a welcome distraction from the crushing acceptance I still had on my plate.

This lady was crying too. Everyone was crying. It was ringing out and echoing like we were at a *STOMP* concert. By the time the staff had taken their seats at the tables in front of the room, it was like being at a mass funeral. It couldn't have gotten any more depressing if they tried. I was expecting a clown to run to the front of the room and shoot himself in the mouth.

I don't remember 95% of this orientation. I don't remember what the principal said. I don't remember what the teachers said. I just remember one guy. Only him. Let me tell you about this one guy.

WELCOME TO THE UNDEFINED WORRY

This man didn't work here. Rather, he was the father of a child in the preschool. As I learned over time, this school enjoyed showing off its advances in overcoming autism. Making non-verbal kids talk was the big achievement they put front and center. Any example that boosted that claim was a notch on their collective belt. Sometimes it felt forced and unneeded. This dude was both of those things.

Mr. Dad was tasked with talking about his personal time with the school. He introduced himself and then proceeded to explain how well his son had been doing since starting classes years earlier. By now, everyone was pretty bummed out, but he was one of us. This was going to be an uplifting tale of redemption and parenthood. I had high hopes this speaker would give us something to remember. Boy did he ever deliver on that.

"*My son has autism. He's non-verbal and he has been working with the school so well these last few years. He had never said a word. At school they work with him on language and learning to get better all the time.*"

If only he had stopped there.

"*I didn't think much of it. Then, the other day, I was in his room and I sneezed. Suddenly I heard a little voice say...*"

And in a high-pitched voice, he continued:

"*Bless you!*"

The whole room shook as if the Pope had just come

parachuting through the skylight. People gasped. Tissue boxes fell. It was like being at a faith healing sermon.

After all, that's what this was. This dude's non-verbal kid spoke! Take my money! That's exactly what so many people in the room were hoping for. This was an actual first-person account of what so many people were hoping for. I was one of those people.

Unfortunately, I knew immediately what had happened. His face told a different story. The moment the audience lit up over the claims of sneezy speech, you could sense that he knew he had made a mistake. There was no smile or nod to acknowledge our excitement. He nervously glanced over at the teachers with a stunned expression. It was like your buddy telling you he has a new girlfriend but she lives far away and you'll never meet her. Then you ask him to call her up in front of you. It's that face. The got-caught face. The my-far-away-girlfriend-isn't-real face.

My head was in so many different directions that I don't remember why they even allowed the crowd to ask this guy questions. It was either part of a Q&A session or an impromptu response to their shock at his story. Why they decided to do autism preschool orientation as if it was a Comic Con panel is beyond me, but minus the Thor costumes, it was. People were able to call out and ask the speakers about their claims of speaking. Of course, someone asked the magic question.

"Does your son talk now?"

"No. He doesn't talk."

"Did he say 'bless you' again?"

"No. Just that one time."

The audible gasp had turned into an audible sigh. It was another letdown and the worst possible thing that this school could have done. Once sitting tall in his chair, the dad had shrunk to half his size. His head hung and the inflection in his voice had flipped.

Even though I was unhappy with his exaggeration, I got why he did it and felt horrible for him. As a father in his position, I couldn't imagine sitting up there and talking to a desperate group of people about such a sensitive subject. His kid was, at most, six years old.

It's hard enough to be honest with yourself about your child's progress at that age. It's almost impossible to do it with a group of people that big. The worst part was that this group of people needed honesty more than ever.

This is the truth, and not a criticism of this father. Ironically, it wasn't until my son was at the same point as this guy's son, ready to graduate from that same preschool years later, that I learned that lesson myself.

He never obtained verbal language there, but Lucas had reached other milestones and enjoyed the school. Still, speech remained the big box that we needed to check.

When the final days of classes came around, we had to answer all the standard questions for the standard people to send him up to kindergarten.

The meeting happened at my home and I found myself sitting at my dining room table with the woman from administration and our coordinator. As papers shuffled and forms were filled out, I was asked if Lucas spoke.

Both I and his coordinator said "no." Then, for some reason, a thing in my brain said, "No. Screw this."

"Actually, he said hi."

I got the same reaction as the dude at orientation, only with less people. The administrator was confused and my coordinator was surprised. They both stared at me.

When pressed for more information, it sounded ridiculous coming from my mouth.

"Yeah. Like last week, I said 'Say hi.' And he did like 'Hhhhhhh.' Like a breath that was almost like, if you listen it was 'hi' but without the 'i' sound. Kind of like 'hi' but only 'H.' You know?"

My coordinator then gave me the only solid advice I can remember her giving. She said it in a sympathetic, albeit condescending, tone.

"Hey. I know what you're doing. That's great and you should definitely tell people about things like that when he does them.

This isn't the place for that. Just the solid stuff so that we can get him the help he needs."

I nodded and put my head down. She was right. For this meeting and many after, I had to keep it in mind when talking about the things Lucas was genuinely able to do. If they don't know where he needs help, they can't help him. If I do something to stop him from getting the help he needs, I'll have failed him as a father.

Pride as a parent has to be put to one side in order to do what's best for your child, especially during the early years when you know them best. That includes admitting truths, accepting help, and being open to alternate forms of communication or learning.

That's something to remember. Any parent who stands in the way of assistance that can make their child into a better adult is doing wrong by their child. Pride, ego, and denial are terrible traits when handling your own affairs. Allowing them to play a role in major decisions for one's son or daughter is unforgivable.

Professionals will always give you hope at the end and you can hang your hat on that, if you want. Every report for my son's future goals begin with "Lucas is a happy, pleasant boy with a great smile and wonderful personality." Then it launches into the 400 things he's not doing. The goal is not to hurt your feelings or downgrade who your child is; the goal is to be realistic about who they are.

It's like the Christmas present thing. Saying Lucas doesn't

like presents is the same as saying he doesn't know how to use a spoon properly. It's just part of who he is. I'm not pretending for anyone because I'm not ashamed. I'm especially not ashamed when I know it can get him the help to reach those goals by admitting it to those who can offer that assistance.

That said, I've learned to appreciate that "anything is possible" mentality. No one knows anything for sure, and the future is never written before you live it. You just have to do what you feel is right. As I often say, I talked to Lucas when I didn't think he understood. I read to him when I didn't think he was listening. I loved him when I didn't think he knew the concept of love.

Because of that, I know today that he understands, listens, and loves me. For a father who wasn't sure of any of that, it makes all the difference in the world. It also requires a leap of faith.

This goes for everything he does. Often with my son things are rough until they're not. He doesn't send us an email or make an announcement. He just takes a hard turn.

CHAPTER 8

Observing, Evolving, Understanding

Learning New Strategies

My best example has to do with his fuzzy noggin. Lucas has a full head of hair and has had since the day he plopped out. It grew finer and thinner when he was little, but it was always in abundance. Getting it cut became a priority early, and, as one might guess, he hated it.

Haircuts became outside-the-house nightmares. Our little Round Mound of Sound would lose his mind before the clipper even touched his cranium. Lucas's mom would come back from the appointments with a little half-cut mohawked mess of a man, and we'd have no idea how to groom this little Tasmanian Devil.

So, we found an "autism-friendly" stylist right smack in one of Long Island's ritzy neighborhoods. This time, Daddy would take him. Maybe a different parent and an understanding barber could work to get him styling and profiling.

Before anything, I have to explain something I've learned. There is no requirement an establishment has to meet to call themselves "autism-friendly." I think the only thing they need to do is not hit people with autism. Even then, I don't think anyone's checking. In other words, "autism-friendly" is like saying "limited time offer." It's nonsense.

Sound cynical? Well, you would be too if you went into this claustrophobic little boutique salon and passed by the ornery receptionist. Ripped right from a Pixar movie, all she needed was a cigarette and antlers.

I told her our name and she sent us into the maze of fire truck seats that were all very cramped for my growing boy. Lucas was giving me a hard time just getting to his seat. I should have known at that point that we were driving one of those trucks straight into an inferno.

To give you an idea of how unfamiliar I was with Lucas's autism at three and the way that others knew how to handle it, listen to what I did next. I put my son in the fire engine and stepped back to allow the stylist to work her autism magic.

Immediately, Lucas held his head...and she didn't know what to do. Every time that she attempted to bring the buzzer close, he put his hand over the spot. Rather than do some musical thing or whatever the hell I figured she was trained to do, she simply dropped her hand to the side and looked away with frustration. This went on for a few minutes. I didn't like it.

The longer it played out, the more ridiculous it became. Still clinging to the hope that she had some sort of specialized technique up her sleeve, I was apprehensive to get involved. Yet, with each passing minute of watching my son uneasy, it felt like a buzzer to the heart. I stepped up and finally helped her hold his hands down.

What followed was a chaotic 10 minutes of physically restraining my kid while a stranger traumatized him. Lucas screamed like we were feeding his fingertips to the wolverines, and I couldn't wait for it all to end.

Then, in the middle of the battle, I looked up to see the hairstylist over my shoulder. She had made contact with the crotchety old front desk lady. When she did, she bugged her eyes out and let out a silent exaggerated sigh. It took all the effort I had to not "accidentally" elbow her in the head.

Instead, I finished this most unfortunate of afternoons and took my crewcut kid home. I vowed to never return.

So, you might assume that my son looks like Cousin Itt now. He doesn't. Lucas's haircut routine switched from the salon to my bathroom, and with that, our outside-the-house nightmare moved inside-the-house.

My boy would be even more wild behind closed doors. There was no cooperation or change in his volatile reaction. The only way I could do it would be to physically wrap my double-jointed legs around his arms as we sat on the floor and try to get him cut as quickly as possible with a dangerous cutter. It was an amateur wrestling match that allowed sharp weapons.

These haircuts killed me. I would say that they took a piece of my soul every time. I hated doing them, and one day, in a fit of anger, I refused to do anymore. I made a huge to-do about it. I went nearly three months, and by the time I finally relented, he looked like one of the Monkees.

Prior to that, I tried everything. Outside of "autism-friendly" salons, there are products for home use that promise to help those on the spectrum too. For Lucas's haircuts, we tried them all.

There was a quiet buzzer that cost $70. There was a pair of scissors that came with a sizing guide. That one was slightly different than the buzzer because it also cost $70... but didn't work at all. We even tried doing it in his sleep as so many people suggested. I cut off one strand before he woke up and looked at me as if I was O.J. Simpson.

Do you know why none of those things worked? It was because Lucas didn't care about sounds. He has no auditory sensory issues. I've seen him fall asleep underneath fireworks. The loudness of the buzzer meant nothing to him. Eventually, I discovered his real issue. It was the way the buzzer pulled on his hair that bothered him.

How do you handle that? Well—get this—you have to cut his hair more often.

Seriously. I figured it out when I went into his three-month Monkee hairdo and he lost his mind each time the buzzer tugged on his strands. I could feel it physically pulling, and matching it up to his reaction, I knew that was causing him problems. It was the length, not the sound.

I'm not sure how I would have ever realized that. After all, my kid hates haircuts on a level most can't comprehend. Why would I give him *more* haircuts? It sounds nuts.

For the first few cuts following that return to form, he was his usual grumpy self. Then, one day, everything changed.

I started his haircut that day, as I do all others, putting his beloved iPad on the counter and turning it on. He stands by it and I come in with the buzzer. It is almost always met with a fall to the floor.

Except that day. He stood tall...without a scream, grab, or squirm. That went on for the whole cut. Lucas was cool, and since that day, he's been fine. It all just stopped. He is over it.

I credit the more consistent haircuts for this transition to haircut acceptance on his part. But if I'm being honest, his maturity was really more important. In the years that followed from that first wrestling match on the bathroom floor, Lucas realized something very important.

He realized that I love him and I wouldn't purposely lead him somewhere that can hurt him.

That's a big deal. It's the most important thing I ever had to teach my son. It's cut down on meltdowns and aggression in substantial ways. It's an aspect of our lives that I once feared he would never understand.

CHAPTER 9

Building Bridges of Understanding

Teaching Trust through Everyday Moments

Every single day, I witness the importance of teaching Lucas to trust me. There were times that I reacted to him in ways that sent the opposite message. They are actions I had to be conscious of and change.

I mentioned earlier that I am unsure if my son understands the concept of special days or even days at all. The same can be said for time. When Lucas first started requesting food with his device, he would routinely ask for pizza. So I'd pop one out of the freezer and start it in the oven.

And he'd whine.

At that point, Lucas would be shooed from the room. I'd simply lead him to the basement to go play, knowing that dinner was on the way. I might tell him that dinner was coming but, at a young age, he didn't know what that meant. He just knew he was being sent away.

It would cause him to launch into a flailing fit and I'd find myself having to comfort him. A voice in my head blamed autism. I'd tell myself that it was just a byproduct of having a non-verbal child.

It's not.

It's the byproduct of having a child who doesn't feel understood. Lucas felt pushed off because that's exactly what I was doing. He felt misunderstood because that was the message I was conveying.

It took so long to get the point to him that food doesn't cook immediately. It was dependent, for me, on hand motions like "stop" and "wait."

These two were longtime favorites already. I would place my hand in front of me to symbolize "stop" and say, in an exaggerated tone, "wait!" It was a motion that I had already started and usually elicited laughter from him because of the voice I used. Now we were using it to make him aware that things take time.

Doing this helps our relationship and saves our evenings. He doesn't melt down over unanswered requests anymore. When it comes to asking for things, he always feels acknowledged. The way I go about handling his needs has changed. I simply try to picture the situation from his point of view.

What would I want? If I didn't have words, how would I know that this person will feed me?

Sure, it's a bit of cheating because Lucas and I have plenty of gestures and receptive language to work with now. He understands more words and movements. So I will turn to him and, through Hulk Hogan-like levels of pantomime, explain.

"**Lucas. No** *(wagged fingers)* **food** *(hand to mouth)* **yet. Wait** *(hands up).* **You play downstairs** *(point to basement door).* **Then...aaaaafffter** *(rainbow motion),* **we eat** *(hands to mouth).* **Okay?**"

Nine times out of ten, he walks away happy. That last time, he makes a whining noise, but still walks away. He may be a scutch, but the days of flailing are behind us.

Now wait *(hands up).* I know what you're thinking. "That's so stupid. He has receptive language and knows those hand motions. That's not a kid who doesn't understand. How do you teach a kid who doesn't understand?"

Well, I did that too. There was a time that he didn't know what any of that meant. Before wagging fingers and rainbow motions, we had to get to a place where he knew what it all meant. Back then I handled it differently.

I showed him the food.

Oh, and he wanted to see it. He still does sometimes. My untrusting little man comes trotting over, takes my hand,

and brings me to the oven. There, I have to turn the light on or open it up to show him that it's on its way.

When he sees it, he will double tap my shoulder to show his approval and walk off. I tell him he's my little supervisor. He needs a clipboard.

Once my Doubting Thomas gets an eyeful, I remind him that I tell the truth.

"See? You have to wait (hands up)**. We have to cook it. Okay? Eat** (hand to mouth) **soon. I promise."**

Then, I keep that promise. That's how he learned that when Daddy says he's got it, Daddy's got it. And Dad's always got it.

Of course, I'm not infallible (don't tell anyone). So, moments where that trust can be tested spring up. I'll forget to fill a cup of juice or get his iPad charged in time. Things like that happen.

When they do, I try my best to help him understand. It's never a simple, "Sorry, pal. No can do." Rather, I work to show him why his device isn't powering on or show my apologies through gestures for his empty cup. I acknowledge my mistakes and let him know that it's not that he's being misunderstood.

It's that things spring up, Dad gets busy, and I'm not actually Superman (I told you not to tell anyone).

This is one of the most important things he's ever needed

to learn. I take Lucas to many places and most of them are new experiences, but even a former stomping ground like the local bowling alley seems new each time out if you don't constantly go. Bringing him from the car into an unfamiliar building used to be like marching him to the electric chair.

He'd fight to stay in the car and then lay down in the parking lot. Gravel would get pushed into his hands, and by the time we stepped through the front door, he was a dirty, gravelly, crying mess.

Five minutes later, he'd be eating pizza and happily rolling a ball. My knee would be bleeding. Fun times. Little bugger.

Today, there are fewer fights to go into a new place with him. The occasional stiff-legged pull-back occurs when leading him by the hand, but that's expected. Overall, going into any location with him is a reminder of how much my boy trusts me now. His only apprehension is laziness and not wanting to get off the soft cushions in my Jeep. It has nothing to do with worrying that I'm taking him somewhere bad.

That means the world to me. It's like watching his face light up over something I did for him. I know that I'm doing things right on a path that I never thought I could navigate.

After all, that's the secret to life. Find someone whose smile makes you happy and then spend the rest of your life making them smile.

CHAPTER 10

Rage, Restraint, and Raising a Non-Verbal Son

Navigating Masculinity in SEN Parenting

There's a scene in *Goodfellas* where Ray Liotta is talking about how his girlfriend's boss complains about her work. The scene immediately morphs into chaos, as you see Ray and the gang destroying the petrified boss's office and screaming, "Janice does whatever she wants!"

That's me with my kids. Every time I hear a bad report or a cross word, I want to launch into full gangster mode and start burning down buildings in fits of rage. Do you know whose kids these are? James's kids do whatever they want!

Unfortunately, I can't do that stuff, so I don't. Legally, it's frowned upon. Also, it makes your kids grow up to be jerks. Can't have any of that.

Still, we're all proud of our own kids. That's the driving force behind that aggressive reaction. You take joy in your kids, seeing them as an extension of yourself. If anyone says anything else, then they get stomped like De Niro.

It's part of what made having Lucas so difficult. This boy is mine. The doggone boy is mine. He was my only son, and I knew that sending him out into the world one day could bring out terrible people. I knew the people who were out there, and I hated the idea of having their judgmental eyes on him.

It was just one of many layers of stress that came about during those early years. I felt I had failed my kid right from the start. If I didn't figure out how to "fix this," then I'd have to accept the fact that I am the one who handed him a life of pain and sadness. I'm a terrible person.

Years later, I know the truth. Having a non-verbal son isn't the end of the world. I have one and he's the center of it. I didn't know that then, though. I didn't know *anything* about special needs then. Without anything playing out, I had no understanding about what autism would be like for our family. All I had was anticipation and heartburn.

People weren't supportive during this time. Most parents in my position have stories of families falling short and friends falling off. Going through an autism diagnosis is not a time for group hugs. It's a time for questions you can't answer, loved ones second-guessing whatever you tell them, and facial expressions you can't handle.

One of the most annoying things I remember was this one family member who I only saw at holidays. He would come over and offer Lucas a high five while he was in his high chair. He did this at every party, every time. He'd come wobbling by and silently stick his hand up for a slap.

My son would ignore him, like he did everyone at the time. That was Lucas's thing. I kid you not. We once met Barry "Greg Brady" Williams of TV's *The Brady Bunch*, who came over and knelt down next to my boy's stroller. He got all Johnny Bravo on him and Lucas, in classic Lucas form, looked past him and over to me with an expression that said, "Who is this doof?"

So when my son would inevitably ignore this virtual stranger in the kitchen, the family member would turn his head and stare at me as if I had done something wrong. I guess the suggestion was that I forgot to teach him high fives. I don't know. It was weird and annoying.

At first, I was embarrassed. I'd take my son's hand and guide him into the high five, along with a nervous laugh.

"Ha ha. Like that, buddy. That's how you five."

After a year or so of this stupidity, I would just shrug and say that he wasn't into high fives.

By two years in, I didn't say anything. I let them stare. That became a theme as my son became older. Let them look. Ya'll go on and look. Just keep your mouth shut.

When it comes to his shortcomings and perceived disabilities, I try not to be defensive to the eyes from family, friends, and the "Harper Valley PTA" wandering through my town. It makes sense that it draws some attention. Luckily, autism awareness has helped families like mine. His actions, for the most part, are understood.

I fully accept that my boy might have tendencies that strangers don't understand. Because of that, I try to be accepting of a glance in our direction. As long as someone isn't gawking or making a pity face, they can look over all they want.

Of course, there are times when you have to stand up. I've had tipping-point moments of frustration, especially in the earlier years. Sometimes people who should stay on the sidelines enter our endzone. That's when you need to punt them back to where they belong.

Lucas was barely three when we embarked on what would become our last cruise. It didn't take long for us to see that cruises seemed like an adventure best suited for our pre-parenting days, free from the burdens of kiddie luggage and accommodating a non-verbal child with autism. Getting my overstimulated son to fall asleep in a room barely the size of a prison cell, when we could barely do it at home, is not something I would ever have chosen on my own.

Oh, and you're rocking back and forth during it. It's like a reality show challenge.

It was clear from the second we pulled out from the docks that many onboard activities weren't designed for children like Lucas. My daughter could participate and enjoy the days of painting shells or whatever the hell they did, but Lucas was often left out. It was a true sign that we may have made the wrong choice, fueling a persistent guilt that I was failing to make his experiences joyful.

On one of the final days, we found small solace in the kiddie sprinkler area of the ship's pool. Lucas was visibly delighted, splashing in the water spouting out of SpongeBob SquarePants. Watching his happiness momentarily lifted my spirits. We were finally relaxed, minding our own business, and watching his sister dart through water streams, when the outside world reared its ugly head.

A boy, maybe ten years old, approached us. He had been playing nearby, roughhousing without consequence. Then he came up to me and Lucas's mom.

"He just splashed me," the little interloper complained, pointing an accusatory finger at Lucas.

This kid was absurd. Not only had Lucas been in our eyesight the whole time, splashing gently in place, but we were also surrounded by cascading water from all directions. It was a sprinkler area. Water was splashing around us. This wasn't a wading pool; it was a giant shower. Even if my boy had done what this kid said—which he hadn't—splashing was the whole point of this area.

Yet this kid singled out Lucas, perhaps seeing an easy target in a child who couldn't argue back. My inner Ray Liotta came out to play.

"Yeah? He probably doesn't like you," I said, meeting this little dipstick's eyes with a stare cold enough to send him scurrying away.

In moments like this, I hear Brad Pitt in *Fight Club* asking me, "Where'd you go, psycho boy?"

At that moment, my words were a knee-jerk reaction, a defensive strike against a perceived threat to Lucas's rare moment of joy. Leave my kid alone.

We all have times like that. It wasn't my finest hour, but still something I take a strange sense of pride in. In keeping with the *Goodfellas* theme, I quote Benny Batz. What's right is right. Now go get your shine box.

Here's my secret to keeping those altercations to a minimum—I watch Lucas closely. Nine times out of ten, my boy is almost always the most well-behaved kid wherever he is with me. I comfort him when he's upset and I take him somewhere quiet if he causes a commotion in a quiet setting. Essentially, Lucas doesn't bother anyone. So if you have a problem with him, then it's because you're a jerk. We deal with those people accordingly.

He was only about three on that cruise and I was struggling with many emotions back then. Life goes on. We grow and evolve. I wouldn't say something like that to a kid now.

Actually, that's a lie. I probably would. For the sake of the segue, though, just go with it. Blah, blah, blah. Times change. Next paragraph.

People never seemed to understand the combination of emotions that accompany a parent's early days of undefined potential "delays" in a young child. The confusion, guilt, and brooding anxiety all form a knot that sits firmly in your stomach. Every aspect of it is painful and nearly impossible to truly explain to a person who hasn't experienced it.

CHAPTER 11

Hello? Anyone There?

The Struggle to Find Support
as a Special Needs Dad

Today, Lucas has autism and he's non-verbal. That's a fact that we can say out loud. It's just a thing. The problem is that there wasn't a moment where a switch goes off and you know for sure. He doesn't suddenly get a membership card or a "This-is-it!" proclamation. Even a diagnosis is given with the hope that "but anything can happen." For parents like me, it's a slow burn that you just sort of live through and hope to come out the other end. It's a treadmill that never stops.

My son's birthdays coincided with annual deals for God. As his second birthday approached, I swore that if he didn't talk by three, it would be cause for concern. Then at three, it was four. At four, it was five. I just kept doing it.

Five, however, was the year that I stopped making deals. I had reality gaveled into my head when he was five. You'll never guess who made me accept that reality.

HI WORLD, I'M DAD

Judge Judy.

You're probably thinking, "Oh. You know Judge Judy?" No. I don't. Never met her, yet she beat me up in my kitchen.

One of my biggest fears during those uneasy times was that someone would say something to throw my world into a tailspin. In the same vein as the jerky kid who screamed "Lucas doesn't talk" at our second birthday party, another situation could arise to knock a realistic point of view into me, and I secretly worried about how I would handle it.

That's what happened one evening while I was making dinner. I was cutting up chicken on the counter while my then-seven-year-old daughter was hovering around. During those times, I'd try to put something distracting on my iPad, but had to make sure it didn't have terrible things on it.

A tip for people with young kids—when you have a seven-year-old, every show in the background is inappropriate. The best I could do was Judge Judy's courtroom. I propped my tablet with everyone's favorite adjudicator up on the stovetop as I cut fat from chicken parts beside it.

I couldn't tell you what the case was about. That isn't just because time has gone by either, but because I was barely paying attention. I rarely did. The most I'd do is pop my head up when she became annoyed and say, "Oooo! You go, Judge Judy!"

So here I am, happily chopping a piece of poultry while Judy's presiding over a case about nothing. All I know is the defendant is shuffling papers and stumbling words. The Judge's face said it all. Annoyed, she began questioning the poorly prepared litigant.

"Madam! You were late returning from work and left the child! How old is the child!?"

The flustered woman trying to organize her documents eeked out a meek "Five." She then added that her child had delays. I kept chopping.

If I had been paying more attention, I'd know why this made Judy angry, but I wasn't and I don't. All I know is that she pressed the woman for information about her child's "delays." The mom then told her that the child didn't speak. My ears perked up just in time for Judge Judy to slam her hand on the desk with defiant punctuation.

"Madam! If the child is five years old and does not speak, that is more than a delay!"

We had just lost cabin pressure. And with that, Judge Judy kicked me in the stomach.

That changed everything for me. Standing there, knife in hand, I stopped making deals, stopped calling Lucas's lack of speech a "delay," and started looking at what we genuinely had going on. I had to pay attention and say "autism" out loud. This wasn't a secret anymore. This was my son. Judge Judy knew, and she hadn't even met him.

I wanted to know him better and I wanted the world to

know him too. Admitting that there were things I was still learning about my son was a big first step towards introducing him to the world.

The big misconception about special needs parents to young children is that any trepidation behind bringing them around family and friends is because of embarrassment. That early isolation period comes off like I am ashamed of my son and unable to accept his disabilities, especially when he's still small.

While that might be true for some people, it wasn't for me. Don't get me wrong. I didn't want anyone mocking him or thinking badly of him. I had already prepared myself for street fighting anyone who did. Trust me. I had entire scenarios planned out in my head where I fight teams of ninjas. In them, I knew parkour and had deadly sword skills.

No. Keeping him away from people wasn't because I feared what *they* would say. It wasn't about what anyone would say except me. To put it more plainly, it was about me and what I *couldn't* say. It was like the high-five guy at Christmas. It was about not knowing things I was supposed to.

I didn't know why Lucas did many of the things he did and I didn't know what he thought about, well, anything. I couldn't offer a genuine response to routine inquiries about my boy, and for that, I was ashamed.

Stop to think about how that makes a parent feel. This was my only son. He'd come toddling out by my side and inevitably someone would ask, "Does he like his teacher?"

"Ummm...?"

"Does he have any friends at school?"

"Uh...?"

"Does he know Santa's coming?"

It killed me. Parents of kids Lucas's age knew everything about their kids. They sang songs together and had favorite TV shows. I couldn't even tell them if my kid liked school. Can you feel that hit you in your stomach? Judge Judy, take me away.

People would say ridiculous things, too. You'd get advice you didn't want and points of view that made no sense. Loved ones you genuinely love can say mind-blowing things. One older family member, who really thought she had cracked the case, suggested that my son's walking delay was because I picked him up too much.

I said, "No. I pick him up because he doesn't walk, not the other way around. If I didn't pick him up, he'd still be sitting in the living room back at my house and miss the barbecue."

Luckily, I had a strong community of support around me. It was easy to get the sympathetic care that I needed during this devastating time. I had the opportunity to discuss my feelings and find camaraderie among others like me. It was a life-saver.

LOL. Just kidding. I'm a man.

Yup. Nothing—especially back then. If you want to feel alone during the loneliest of times, be a dad. Every meme, every show of support, and every community event is structured towards supermoms. The fathers in all those memes are depicted as sleeping, confused, or barely interested. If they simply stay around, it's treated as some bizarre outcome.

It wasn't any better offline. I didn't have other special needs dads to talk to because...well, I never saw any of them. We knew the moms for years. The dads were a name and an occasional appearance.

Even in the years that followed, I've barely seen any fathers. That's not to say they're not active in the lives of their children. That's not the point I'm making, although I'm not sure either way. I'm just saying they don't bake casseroles and come over for a good cry with other fathers. We just float along. The support circle isn't too wide for dudes. It's less of a circle and more like a line. A line with one person.

To occupy my mind, I played a lot of *Call of Duty®* during those darker days. People hear that and say, "You must really like *Call of Duty®*." I do not. I played it because it would last 10 intense minutes, the round would end for a minute, and it would start up again. Whenever I decided to play, I could eat my life up in 10-minute spurts on my mad dash to the finish line. Turn on, tune in, drop out.

As for words of inspiration, I didn't have that. Instead, I listened to grown men argue with children over Xbox headsets. In some cases, a person would scream or sing. I was once in a room where one dude would just pick an offensive word and repeat it forever. I kid you not. I muted him and came back half an hour later and he was still doing it. Those were my words of support.

Honestly? It helped, I guess. My goal was to get my mind off of things, and that seemed to do the trick. As I came to find out through the years, support for dads runs low, and that's not limited to the early years or even kids with special needs.

CHAPTER 12

Make Room for Daddy

Confronting Professional Bias and Embracing My Role as a Hands-On Dad

In a world where equality and true balance should exist, most men are treated as the lesser parent. If you think it's justified because so many men take off, then your thinking is part of the problem. Maybe consider that the lowered expectation bar for dads is why disinterest seems like an acceptable option to some. It's not an option to me. These are my kids. I'm not going anywhere—physically or otherwise. I have just as much of a right to them as their mother does. We're equals in their eyes.

Yet, it doesn't feel that way. To view it through the eyes of the gatekeeping masses, you'd think a man's role is to be a glorified child. It's as if the world gets its views about a man's place in society from an 80s sitcom. I'm not that guy. I don't ask where mommy keeps the peanut butter or iron you a grilled cheese sandwich. Proudly, I'm an adult, and running my own house includes knowing how to care for the people I love the most. I set an example and handle my responsibilities. There are many dads out there like me.

Once, I had one of our early intervention therapists commend me for my fathering. She added:

"Many fathers can't accept their child having a delay."

Her words took me back for a moment. I could understand the gist of what this statement meant, but it didn't sit well for a few reasons.

For starters, many mothers can't accept delays either. I've seen the spectrum of denial across a number of different people. From mothers who tell stories of their children reading or writing when many know they can't to dads who completely duck out on their parental responsibilities. The idea of caregivers not caring sounds like a paradox, but sadly, it's a reality.

The other part of this statement that got me is that, while I remember struggling with the idea that my boy might face delays in life, I never knew that not accepting it was an option. This is my son. I made him and he needs me. How is simply saying "nope" to the person he is a viable response?

Maybe it was all that swirling in my head or my defensive nature at the time, as it related to Lucas. Either way, I replied and it kind of shook the room.

"'Fathers can't accept' it? What exactly does that mean?"

She froze. I guess no one had asked her that before. Sure, it sounds innocent, but is it? She didn't know how to answer.

"They just can't accept it."

So I helped her along.

"You're saying they leave?"

I had made things uncomfortable for her. Me? I was fine. She offered another half-shrug.

"Yes, some of them do."

"Well, thanks. I'm not going to leave my family."

People have heard that story and seen it from other angles. I get that she didn't mean anything by it, but doesn't it speak to her opinion on a father's role in the family when simply not abandoning them is seen as something to applaud? No one ever told Lucas's mom that. No one tells any mom that.

There's nothing worse than being up with your non-verbal child all night as he fights you to stay awake, only to go online and see memes about how dads do nothing. Imagine being half-asleep from a night of battles with your kid and then having to read about how a woman takes care of her kids while her husband sleeps like a baby.

8 million likes. U go mama #forthekiddos

During those times, all the little images with words feel

like they're exclusively for the moms. It's a slap in the face to every father and every single dad who takes an interest in their children—autism or otherwise.

I speak from experience. I'm a single dad myself, but even before the divorce, I took on the lion's share of my son's care. I attended all his school meetings and back-to-school events, often alone. The fact that I was a man didn't stop me from making sure my special needs child's needs were attended to.

In fact, that whole "be a man" routine that society used to push when I was a kid holds through. Is there anything more "manly" than making sure your loved ones, especially the most vulnerable, are cared for? Man up, Dad.

Today I have split custody, right down the middle, and I am tasked with caring for Lucas when he's with me. That means those early morning wake-ups and anxiety-inducing schedule juggles fall on me too.

Part of being the solo caregiver, though, is taking up the reins that you might otherwise leave to your spouse. That's what happened when I was put into a text group for my son's class. After learning that we had accidentally missed the deadline to contribute to a class gift, I made a point to enter the group myself. There were six people in the class and six in the group. It was supposed to be about class teacher gifts and field trips. I figured it was important. I didn't realize how quickly it would morph into much more.

Memes, gossip, questions about nothing. I found myself

routinely muting the group chat, but then jumping back to check and make sure I hadn't missed something important. I offered comments on all the impending decisions and voted for nonsense, like whether to get a Starbucks gift card or a flower bouquet. It was dumb.

The worst part? The mom who crowned herself the leader felt the need to begin all her messages with, "Hello ladies."

This Val Venis-like opening didn't sit well with me, but I tried to ignore it for a while. I even ignored the asides from the other five moms who would also always overlook that there was a dad in the group. If one person would say something like "Don't mess with our kiddos" another would respond, "Or their moms!" I'd usually put a question mark reaction to it. No one cared.

Eventually, I did say something about these daily gender-exclusion greetings to the top mom. Of course, she was super-embarrassed. It immediately stopped and everyone apologized.

Ha ha. No. I'm kidding. It didn't. They just kept doing it.

Eventually, I left the group in a fit of annoyance. I heard from another mom later that year that the "Hello ladies" Lady said, "Well, he knew it was a mom's group text when he joined it." Point taken. Bye, Felicia. No more $20 for munchkins from me.

It basically takes that feeling of isolation, something all special needs parents face, and compounds it for a man.

Yet, both parents deal with it pretty substantially. It's something moms and dads can both relate to.

My approach has never been to cry about the challenges we face. Instead, I've focused on celebrating the unique ways autism has shaped Lucas. His laughter fills our good days, which significantly outnumber the tough ones. Life with Lucas isn't defined by phases but rather by the overwhelming presence of an extraordinary human being.

However, those early days weren't filled with celebration. I didn't know what to celebrate, what our lives would look like, and if this aspect of our family—one that still had yet to fully play out—would destroy us. I didn't want to say it out loud, much less confide in others. It didn't matter anyway. I had no one to tell, even if I wanted to. Those I could tell wouldn't understand anyway. No one did.

Communicating the complexities of our life was far from straightforward. We're invisible to the outside world until an unexpected meltdown or outburst reveals a different reality.

"How do you manage?" people wonder, their words a mix of admiration and pity. Back then, I found myself wondering the same. I didn't know how I was doing or if I'd be able to do it through the years. The memes said I couldn't, but I knew I had no choice. I owed it to Lucas and I still do. I owe it to him for the rest of his life.

CHAPTER 13

Entering His World, Redefining Mine

The Journey to Acceptance and True Connection with My Son

My parenting journey has been a spectrum of trials and errors. In Lucas's younger days, typical disciplinary tactics like time-outs or stern talks fell flat. They simply didn't connect with him. The most frustrating moments couldn't even be met with a frustrating response. He'd absorb my annoyance and then continue doing whatever it was that I warned him against. It was pretty maddening for a father. Have you ever had a kid disobey you while making eye contact and you know that he's not doing it on purpose? I have. I had it when he was small. I had it yesterday. It happens all the time.

It took years to evolve from a frustrated dad to one who sits patiently by his son's side during a public meltdown. Understanding Lucas means recognizing the invisible burdens we carry. Outsiders rarely see the constant balance of managing his immediate needs while planning for his future. Their fleeting glances don't catch the endless calculations running through my mind. Parenting my son is a constant balance of planning out today, tomorrow, and the years to come. Time is truly a flat circle and all these concerns occur concurrently.

Often, the hardest misunderstandings come not from strangers but from those closest to us. It is shocking when family and friends, those expected to be our staunchest supporters during the uncertain years, fall terribly short. They don't see the early mornings filled with chaos or the late nights running through doomsday scenarios in my head.

I've heard it all from the people you'd least expect to falter. "Everyone has problems," they'd dismiss. "Well, you chose to have kids," they'd say, as if Lucas was a cause for blame, and parenting him was merely a lifestyle option. Some of the coldest responses came from people you'd expect the opposite from. It makes parents feel alone, but it makes them feel their children are even more alone. I barely understood Lucas and I spent my days with him. These people will never know him.

Faced with such emotional isolation, I learned to stop seeking understanding where there was none to be found. I stopped explaining, stopped justifying, and stopped looking for love in the trash. There are those who "get it" and those who never will. The distinction became as clear as day.

That's a hard bridge to cross as we're conditioned to reach out to loved ones, especially during our darkest days. When those loved ones make the darkness darker, though, it's best to find your light somewhere else.

Today, when people commend my patience, it no longer feels like the hollow praise they offered when I was unsure of my place in Lucas's life. I've come to accept it as recognition of a profound truth. Managing life with Lucas isn't about battling through each day; it's about embracing each moment with love. This understanding doesn't come easily to everyone. Some lack the capacity to put someone else's needs before their own, especially when the situation demands unwavering compassion without immediate gratitude.

In a nutshell, Lucas taught me that you don't say hello to someone just to get a hello back. You don't help someone to get a thank you. You show love because you want to, not because you anticipate reciprocity. He's helped me understand what it means to truly be selfless.

Luckily, I've gotten love back from my boy. But I didn't go into it with that expectation. I loved him because I had no choice. It was just a feeling inside me that I felt the moment I saw him.

The journey has taught me that the rewards of learning Lucas far outweigh the effort. Those who fail to see the value in what we experience simply miss out on the profound depth of what it means to truly connect with another person on the purest of levels. In the end, the loss is theirs. For Lucas and me, and for all who truly know us, the journey is rich with rewards that transcend words.

HI WORLD, I'M DAD

As special needs parents, we often feel alone. But through shared experiences and stories, we find community and understanding. If you're walking this path, know that while the journey is challenging, it is also filled with moments of profound joy and connection. Lucas doesn't need words to communicate his love, and as his father, neither do I. Our bond speaks volumes in the silence, in the challenges, and in every small victory along the way.

Yet, when he was little, I didn't know any of that yet. I just knew something was "wrong." It was all I could think about... until an unexpected twist in my story came along. Then, I just stopped thinking about it for a while. I had no choice.

CHAPTER 14

Everything Can Change in a Moment...

Refocusing on What Truly Matters as a Father

When it came to my son's emerging delays, it felt like there was nothing else to think about. Worries about Lucas, then just shy of two years old, plagued me in my waking hours. I would have given anything to be able to focus on something else.

Then, on December 13, 2013, the universe gave me something else.

I was 35 years old and had always been in fairly good health. There was nothing to be concerned about that day when I found myself struggling a bit to catch my breath. As had happened on and off for years, I felt a throbbing pain along my torso and a tingling in my hands.

Many reading right now may have already guessed that I was having a heart attack. Had you told me that at the time,

I would have argued against you. In fact, I was so sure that this was nothing to worry about, I walked myself next door to the emergency walk-in center in the strip mall adjacent to my house...

...as I was having a heart attack.

Yes. That was the day that I learned my "episodes," which always seemed to correct themselves within minutes, had all been heart attacks. There was something seriously wrong.

Once I arrived at the hospital, I learned just how serious they were. My arteries all had substantial blockages, which would have been shocking for someone twice my age. The room went quiet as the doctor began pointing to the grainy display and saying things like 80%, critical, and surgery.

With no history of any surgery in my life, I found out that I needed a quintuple bypass. Shocked, empty, and confused, I asked him if I would need to call to schedule it.

"Call? No, Chief. You're going in tonight."

With that, my world was knocked off its orbit. After a lifetime of worrying about so many things that never happened, here I was about to possibly die from surgery that was never even on my radar. As the doctor continued to babble at my dumbfounded face, he said something that has lived with me to this day.

"You know those guys who walk around perfectly healthy and

then drop dead from a heart attack at 40? That was going to be you."

And like that, I was off to have major surgery and forever alter the trajectory of my life.

I should also mention that, at that point, I was positive I was going to die. I knew nothing about bypass surgery outside the terrifying TV specials I'd seen as a kid. This was major. I was pretty positive I was done.

That's when it all started to sink in. What did I regret most in my final moments? Strangely, my disappointment was specific. It was all the times my children were in the living room watching TV and playing while I sat in my home office refreshing the same internet pages. I was doomscrolling while my favorite people were two rooms away. That was the wasted time that I thought about during, what I believed to be, my final moments. That has stayed with me. People think about what they will look back on and wish they did differently when they are about to die. This was mine. To this day, I still remember that feeling.

All this musing over my own mortality was swirling around in my brain when my surgeon, all decked out in scrubs, came to talk to me. He told me not to worry, and that the quintuple bypass had a 97% success rate. I expressed shock.

"Really? I thought it was like 20 or something!"

I'll never forget the look on his face.

"Why the hell would we do it if it had a 20% success rate?"

He had a point. Still, I thought I was definitely dead, but maybe my consciousness would wake up in another timeline where I'm alive. That sounded good enough for me.

They popped a little translucent blue shower cap on my head and began pushing my stretcher towards the operating room. I remember the spotless corridor and seeing my body in the round corner mirrors of the hallway. The last thing I remember were the double doors opening and a beam of light coming out. The foreboding symbolism wasn't lost on me.

Spoiler alert, I lived. You know that because you're reading this book, but it would have been a hell of a twist if I didn't, huh?

As I recovered from this ordeal, my chest felt like it had a bag of broken glass in it and I couldn't breathe properly for weeks. I was told not to lift my kids or anything over 10 pounds for a few weeks. For the first time in my life, I felt helpless.

People offered me pudding cups and balloons, but all I wanted was to see my children. When I eventually graduated from hell and was moved into my regular room, I was given a framed picture of the two of them. It was from a photo shoot we had taken them to just a few weeks before.

We had gone to one of those fancy photographers at the local mall. Lucas, of course, was on fire. All he wanted to do was run. Eventually, he broke free and I chased him up and down the corridors. The photo, one of my favorites, shows him just a split second before he darted off. To those who don't know that he was seconds from sprinting, he just looks happy. It makes me smile every time I see it.

Oh yeah. Remember that? Lucas has autism.

You may have noticed that my son's autism, splashed from cover to cover here, hasn't been mentioned over the last few pages at all. That same thing happened in life. My boy's emerging so-called disabilities, all of which were constantly on my mind for a year, weren't even in my head until this photograph came to my room days later.

That's because, when it comes to the love I have for my children, those things don't matter. Whatever they are or become is part of a person that I love. I don't love my daughter because she speaks. I love her because she's my daughter. The same thing could be said for my son. Yet, with so much concern for so long, I kept losing sight of that.

When your days are spent Googling ways to "fix" your child, you forget to take notice of who your child is. They just become that thing that you're trying to remedy rather than a beloved family member who has traits and quirks. I had spent so long seeing my son as a problem that needed a place on my checklist as opposed to my wonderful son who I regretted missing even the minor moments with.

This was what made me, for the first time ever, see through the haze of fear about who my boy would become. I saw who he was at that very moment. Rather than mentally flash forward to doom and gloom, I focused on the present, and the present was wonderful.

This was my boy. The fact that he's in my life is all that matters. Just like I didn't need his sister to be a star volleyball player or Scrabble® champion in order to see her worth and beauty, I didn't need him to speak or understand certain things in order to see his. The bonds we create with people aren't about what they do or what they don't do. The bonds we create with people are about who they are.

When I returned home on December 20, 2012, one day before the Maya were supposed to wipe us out, the first thing I did was watch *Rudolph the Red-Nosed Reindeer* with Olivia while Lucas played in the living room. To this day, it is one of my happiest memories. They tell you to take in the great moments when they're happening, and that's what I did.

Even as we were sitting there on December 20th, I was conscious of how close I came to not sitting there on December 20th. That afternoon in my living room was all I could ever want, and I felt lucky beyond words to have the opportunity to live it again.

Since then, a lot has changed. My temperament has gone from easily annoyed to creepily Zen. Stress doesn't get to me the way it used to. I'm very much aware that most things I worried about never came to fruition while an unexpected major heart event almost killed me. Today, I don't sweat the small stuff. Actually, I don't even sweat the big stuff.

My diet and exercise routine has changed and my approach to the world is different too. I'm not always trying to fix the things around me. Rather, I'm trying to learn about what's around me and become a part of it. Lucas was a big part of that, and the prism through which I saw his autism changed tremendously.

No longer was I trying to figure out how to wedge him into our world. Now, I wanted to know about his world. It was time to be the dad he deserved, but first I had to understand what that meant for him.

In the weeks that followed my surgery, I felt helpless. I ate oatmeal and blew into a little tube thing that was supposed to exercise my lungs. All it really did was mock me with my lack of breathing ability.

Like a grandpa on holiday, I sat around my house and just soaked in the world around me. My brain was in a million different directions already.

Not only was I grateful for my George Bailey-esque return to life, but I was now left to wonder how I felt about that life. Was I happy with who I was? What about the stresses that caused me to waste so much time?

One of those stresses was the unknown of Lucas's future. We had long tried to get him to play with toys "the right way." He didn't bang mallets or play with the stupid Music Together scarves. That had driven me crazy in my past life. How had that obsession played a role in my health issues?

How would my life play out going forward without that worry weighing so heavily on my shoulders?

I was in the living room with Lucas on one of those days and, at the time, we lived in a house with way too many mirrors. Like something out of a 50s funhouse, our home had come with reflective walls and sliding doors. For the adults, it was a constant game of plucking and combing. For Lucas, it was reflection party time.

He loved those mirrors and would sit for hours clapping and staring into them. If you tried to pull him away, he'd get upset and crawl back. Take it from me, I took him from them many times in his youngest years. Now, after my surgery, I felt bad that I ever had.

Things were different now and I chalk it up to my new relaxed perspective. While my boy was playing with his toys on this new day, I didn't pull him away or correct his usage. Rather, I watched quietly. Instead of labeling his unorthodox play methods as "red flags for autism," I saw them as his play methods. Nothing more, nothing less. I saw him for who he was.

What Lucas was doing was deliberate and something I had seen him do many times. He had one of those little telephones on wheels. You know the ones with little eyes that open and close as the wheels turn. You pull it on a string. Google it. You know it.

My son was putting the phone under our red easy chair and slowly pulling it back out by its string. When he did, he wouldn't look at it directly. Rather, he'd watch in the mirror with an expression of astonishment. This went on over and over again.

It wasn't just that he did it. It was the intensity with which he watched. He was studying the scene like he was conducting an experiment. While earlier I was preoccupied with the notion of "You don't play with a toy phone like that," now I was stuck on asking, "*Why* does he play with it like that? What is he looking for?"

Lucas's communication skills were still emerging at that point, and there were very few signals we shared. When I sat next to him on the floor, I tried a universal one. I took the string gently in one hand, and, with the other hand, I patted myself on the chest.

"I try?"

Double taps had always been understood and I remember his expression seemed slightly perplexed, but it was fixed on me. It was one of the first times I felt he truly focused on something I was trying to communicate to him besides food or fun. He let me take the toy from him.

Then, with the string in hand, I repeated the same motion he had been doing. I watched in the mirror with the same intensity that he had done earlier. He looked like he couldn't believe someone else was doing this.

Then he stood up and hugged me. I wanted to cry.

That was the day that my son and I started over. We've been moving forward from that one action ever since, and without it, I never would have learned to appreciate him on the level that I have. It was the day I entered his world, and it's the day that he let me.

CHAPTER 15

And a Child Shall Lead Them

Finding Common Ground and Redefining My Role as a Father

Entering Lucas's world means more than simply playing with his toys in the ways he does or watching the same shows he enjoys. It's about finding the common ground between his motivations and mine. It's about understanding that people like him and people like me are strikingly similar.

The differences are easy to spot, but superficial things often are. It's like seeing a person who reacts strongly to football and another who acts the exact same way with baseball. At first glance, you see they're not the same. Take more than a minute to look at their reactions rather than what they're reacting to, and you see the connection.

Lucas and I have similar motivations, loves, and emotions. The only thing that separates us are the instances and objects themselves. A lot of it also has to do with the fact that my son can be open and unfiltered in ways that I strive to emulate.

The truth is, I envy a lot of who my boy is. That's a big part of autism appreciation. It's about recognizing that so much of what makes him who he is are characteristics that mirror my own. He's not a different species; he's a human being. A 13-year-old boy with autism is still just a 13-year-old boy.

That's why I always raise an eyebrow to the phrase, "If you meet one person with autism, you've met one person with autism." I get the meaning behind it and do applaud the sentiment. It's a great way to explain the true length of the spectrum. However, it always struck me as slightly off when you think about it.

That idea isn't specific to autism. It can be applied to anyone. Saying "You meet one person with autism and you've met one person" works better. My son is a person. Everything he does, no matter how strikingly different it seems, is actually straight out of my own brain. Meeting one person with autism doesn't tell you about everyone with autism, just like meeting one boy doesn't tell you about every other boy on Earth. My son is unique because he has autism, but he's also unique simply because he is an individual.

If you're wondering how we can have similarities when our actions differ so much, you just have to look at the reasons why he does the things he does. My son doesn't do things for the sake of doing them. No meltdown, scream, or reaction is for no reason. To dismiss the things Lucas does as being without motivation is to dismiss him out of your own personal misunderstanding.

The clapping and jumping over his iPad? That's an easy one to tie back to me and many others reading this. You think it's strange? Is it? Who the hell doesn't want to clap and jump for joy over their favorite thing? Toyota had an entire 1980s ad campaign devoted to it. Give my son the things he loves and he will beat you to death with how ecstatic he is for it.

That's a beautiful thing. I want that in my own life and heart. I've spent a lifetime chasing that enthusiasm, and year by year, I find myself getting closer because of his example. I watch my son and I'm inspired to find that feeling for myself. Why don't I have it? Sadly, I think I know.

Like many others, I allow the shackles of social judgment to stop me from jumping for joy. Like *Harrison Bergeron*, the chains from society ground my joy. Had it not been for those wet blankets raining on my parades and peeing in my Cheerios, I'd probably be jumping around happily over the things I love too.

Instead, I'm an adult who's somewhat constricted by the same social norms my son is oblivious to. Things I've come to accept as "normal" are far from my instinct. You're supposed to find what you love and react with relentless enthusiasm. It's what we all strive from a friend, family member, partner. It's passion and love. It's who we all want to be.

My son lives that romantic life, wearing his heart on his chewed-up sleeves, and in doing so, reminds me to be alive. I watch him and I admire his approach. If only I could be like Lucas and not care what others think.

This "disability" has led him to approach his own happiness in ways we all wish we could. If only I could have had the same zest for happiness that he has—the same zest that everyone acts so perplexed by—I'd truly be at peace.

My uptick in outward expressions of glee these past few years can be attributed, in many ways, to Lucas. The more I learn about him, the more I want to see the world as he does. If he can open his heart without fear of others, I can do the same thing.

Now, keep in mind this emotional entanglement we share doesn't stop at joy and happiness. We share so much common ground across all his moods. Once you start to see the link of one, you see the link of them all. We're closer to same than not.

For example, if you take me to a boring dinner party, I will endure it. Tell me all about Jerry's Lasik surgery and bore me to tears. I'll still make it to the finish line with a pocketful of shrimp tails. Sure, there are times when I might make a sarcastic comment or an annoyed sound, but I'm usually on my best behavior. Life isn't a Garth Brooks song. You can't go around ruining black-tie affairs.

Well, that's not entirely true. Sure, *you* can't, but Lucas can. Bring my boy to a dinner party he hates and he will eventually lay on the floor in a fit of annoyance. When he was tiny, it would happen immediately. As he's aged and learned to "be a big boy," he deals with it a little longer. Still, wait long enough, and he's face-down under the table whining. Then...he gets to go home and jump for joy over his iPad.

Who doesn't want to do that? Think about it. You're seated across from your in-laws and they're talking endlessly about your future plans and financial decisions. Who wouldn't want to look them in the face and yell out, "Eh-hhh!"? Follow it up with a flailing of your arms that knocks over everything on the table before tossing your body dangerously on the ground. Imagine it. Doesn't it sound wonderful? Don't you wish you could do that right now? I'll give you a moment to imagine it.

The only reason you don't do it is because you've been taught not to. My son has been taught that, as well. It just took a little longer to get him to understand why. While many of us just needed a stern adult to tell us to "cut the crap and be nice because that's what people do," a non-verbal boy takes a bit longer to grasp the concept. I'm sure if he had words, his response would be, "Why?"

And that's where he and I diverge, at times. I get his motivations and I look to his social indifference with a sense of whimsical wonder. However, there are many times when those social rules are there for a reason and I wish he would adhere to them a bit better. I want people to accept him and work to make him see the importance of that. It's part of the balance that comes with being his father.

It's something I put on my shoulders to teach him, even though I understand (and kind of appreciate) his thought process.

CHAPTER 16

Sorry My Kid's Trying to Eat Your Lunch

Food, Eating, and Impulse Control

As my son has grown both physically and chronologically, certain lessons need to be locked down a bit more. For Lucas, the impulse to pillage food from the plates of others is probably one of the biggest ones I can think of.

Since he was old enough to wobble through the house, Lucas has the natural build of a miniature linebacker—sturdy, determined, and ever-ready to bulldoze through any obstacle like the Stay Puft Marshmallow Man. My guy has a natural curiosity about the world around him, especially when it comes to things he can chow down on.

His appetite is legendary in our household. He's not fussy about his meals, happily gobbling up anything from sushi to exotic fruits. Shocking to many who believe that autism means picky eating, Lucas doesn't play that. I've long suspected that the experience of chewing is mostly sensory for him, but either way, he's a total foodie. This unselective palate often leads to some memorable, if slightly mortifying, family moments of impulse control issues.

I've made spinach artichoke dip, only to find he has plunged his hands into the cream cheese base that's cooling in the fridge. I've left sandwiches on the table while getting a soda, only to discover them half-hanging from his chubby little face. I've watched him stuff an entire bagel in his mouth. It's like filming *Ripley's Believe It Or Not* in my dining room.

One of his most famous Hungry Mungry incidents unfolded at my then-nine-year-old daughter's basketball trophy ceremony, held in the cramped multipurpose room of our local church. The event was a typical family affair, chaotic and loud, with parents juggling the tasks of clapping, cheering, and capturing the perfect photo. Stand up. Sit down. It was like church, which, given the setting, felt fitting.

In the thick of these festivities, my attention was momentarily divided between Olivia's achievement and keeping an eye on Lucas. I was concerned he'd dart into the parking lot and get hit by a car. It was pretty much all I worried about whenever I took him anywhere at that age. If we were within a mile of a parking lot, I pictured him getting squished in it.

Luckily, I didn't have to worry about my son disappearing. I had him right there in my sights. As everyone was standing to applaud the next group of kids, I saw my boy hanging out mere feet away.

There he was, one table down, adorable and fervently sucking down a venti iced coffee from Starbucks. He attacked that straw with such gusto that I half-expected him to get sucked into the cup, his face screwed up in intense concentration. It was a funny mental image that made me smile. Aw, how cute my son is. Ha ha ha. My little chubby face boy all stuck in the Starbucks...

Then I stopped short.

And realized that we hadn't gone to Starbucks that day. Even if we did, no one is buying a five-year-old a latte.

Panic set in as I noticed he was standing behind an unsuspecting family, whose matriarch had momentarily left her drink unguarded to applaud her own child. As she turned back to her seat, she was greeted with my little coffee burglar, still swigging away on her drink.

My heart stopped for a moment until her expression morphed from confusion to amusement. Before anyone else could speak, we hurried to apologize. Of course, what do you say to someone whose coffee your son has commandeered and is literally guzzling at that moment? He was caught. He was Goldilocks in Baby Bear's bed and, in typical Lucas form, he didn't care. I couldn't think of what else to say besides "sorry" and "let us pay for it."

"Um, hope you don't have hepatitis?"

No. I didn't say that, but I don't know. I hope she didn't. If she did, we'd know by now, right?

Despite the awkwardness, the woman was understanding. These incidents always remind me of how quick I am to expect judgment, yet people usually surprise me with their kindness. I kind of feel bad about the hepatitis joke now.

Still, it was important to take responsibility and offer payment. In these cases, it would be easy to shrug and just go along with their good-natured autism acceptance. Yet it's important, as a parent, to show that you appreciate compassion towards your child while understanding personal responsibility.

This wasn't the first time Lucas's impulsive nature had led to such a scene, and nor would it be the last. I came to realize that he didn't necessarily have a passion for coffee as much as he was drawn to large, clear cups with their irresistible green straws.

He knows the rules and understands the word "no," but for my little man, at that age, the allure of something he desires can override the boundaries we've set. Again, I can relate to this way of thinking. I think that way too. The only reason I'm not running up to everyone's delicious food choices that I didn't order and grabbing a handful is social restraints. It's also the desire to not get banned from Panera Bread that keeps me on my best behavior.

For Lucas, not so much. This was never clearer than during a holiday classroom activity where we were supposed to decorate pancakes with sweet toppings. My guy, however, had other plans.

Parents were invited to join in and, just like the annual gingerbread house decorating that becomes an hour of him pleading to eat the gumdrops, this felt like a daunting task. It was hard for him to resist eating it and hard for me to stop him. That became the great pancake game.

From the outset, Lucas was visibly frustrated by the delay between making Mr. Pointless-Pancakeface and being allowed to eat him. His decorations were minimalist and his demeanor hangry. Begrudgingly, he made the stupid breakfast decoration with all the enthusiasm of an unenthusiastic pancake decorator. Mr. Breakfast had two small eyes and a Twizzlers smile. Short, sweet, and ready to eat. Have at it, Chubbs Malone.

Once we were done and he was given the go-ahead, my kid devoured the edible project as if he was being neglected at home. After swallowing the two giant bites, this predator of the pancake jungle began immediately eyeing the other children's uneaten creations. I had to firmly tell him "no." Those were not for him. Those were the pancake faces of other kids. Down, Mr. Butterworth. Down.

But Lucas, being Lucas, was unhappy, and I could feel his need to feed growing by the second. I knew that I had to keep close tabs on him and I did. I so did. I had him. I swear. Yet when he saw an opportunity to steal someone else's creation, he did.

In a swift, athletic move that I doubt he could ever repeat, my round little fella went full-scale Superman and dove across two desks. As he flew through the air, he swung his arm and swiped a pancake from another kid's empty seat. Falling to the floor, Lucas stuffed the entire thing into his mouth and triumphantly looked up at me and his teacher.

Maybe it was the fall. Maybe it was carb overload. Most likely he was the sensory overload, but soon his face was full of pancake and tears. It was a terrible scene and one that I didn't know how to handle.

Sometimes, like this time, he gets so overloaded with impulse and emotion that the end result of his behavior doesn't even make him happy. He gets what he wants, and he's still left crying.

It's not naughty; it's uncontrollable. If it was truly naughty, he'd be happy. He wasn't. Watching him cry was like watching a volcano erupt. For every parent who laments over not understanding their kid in times like this, there's a kid who is experiencing it 100 times worse than we could ever imagine. I love my son and hate to see him feel that way. It can break your heart.

Forget being embarrassed that he stole a pancake. Forget being angry that he disobeyed. Forget everything about me and my own place in this situation. This was about Lucas. He was the one who needed me. Even though we were still early on in our journey through his needs, I knew when my boy needed some understanding.

Some impulses are overwhelming, but there are ways to help him get around it. Through the years, I've learned to help Lucas understand what's coming next. He needs to see that he can trust me to get him the things he wants. Today, if he wants a pancake, he can ask in a variety of ways. Most likely, I'll let him have it, if he makes the effort to communicate.

Some kids like him use "social stories." They look like little comics and show, in each box, a step-by-step guide of what's to come. They make them for kids to get ready for school and things like that. While Lucas doesn't really pay attention to them specifically, the idea behind it is one that we have gravitated to. He needs to be kept in the loop. That's what we do.

If he wants a pancake and I don't want him to have one, I don't say "no" and push him off like many would do with a neurotypical child. In Lucas's case, he has no way of knowing if I even understand what he wants. That's why I go out of my way, like I do with food cooking, to show him that he is understood.

Does that mean he always gets what he wants? No. But if I don't want him to have it, I say "no" clearly and understandably. He's learned to accept that. Sure, he might whine or dig his heels in before walking off, but he doesn't freak out like he once would have. The reason why is that he's learned to trust me. He knows that I never steer him wrong or ignore his feelings. If I deny him something, it's for a reason. His needs will be met. His dad has his back.

Showing my kid that he can count on me has been a game-changer as he's gotten older. Lucas has become so much more mature in that sense. Still, I wouldn't leave him alone in a room with my dinner when he's hungry. I may be trusting, but I'm not stupid.

So let's recap the similar feelings. Happy—check. Bored at parties—check. Wanting to steal delectable morsels from others—check. All these things are easily comparable to the motivations I might have throughout the day.

Of course, people will point to some of his other, more inappropriate, traits as being uniquely autism-based. How about getting naked? Like many kids on the spectrum, Lucas goes through phases when he wants to strip his clothes off and run around with his bits and pieces flying about. Nothing like a round underage streaker in the den at 3pm on a Sunday afternoon.

Uh...so how is that autism-based? I want to do that. I want to do that right now. Who doesn't want to run free like a hippie in their own house? It's freeing, and as long as the temperature works, it feels great. Swing it in the breeze, pal.

Body issues? My son has no body issues. He's not even aware that's a thing. Lucas doesn't do crunches or go tanning. Bro don't even lift. Yet he'll show you his abundance of abs whenever the mood hits. I don't know about you, but that's admirable in the big-picture sense. Sure, getting naked isn't good. But knowing he has body positivity is good, right? Come on. It's all the rage.

Lucas does what his heart tells him to do and everything can be boiled down to that. He chews his sleeves when he wants to and he rips his books when he turns the pages of them with more excitement than I've ever devoted to turning a page. If he doesn't want pillows on his bed, he throws them across the room. He closes doors in the faces of people he doesn't want bothering him and asks for water repeatedly even if he's had ten glasses. That's my boy.

In a different life, he would be a high-ranking captain of industry. No one is in tune with their personal wants more than my son and no one gives less of a damn about the opinions of others than he does. My son is the embodiment of every self-help seminar people toss thousands of dollars at. He's centered on a level unlike anyone else.

What I'm saying is that Lucas listens to himself. He knows who he is and he's in tune with his desires. I have never known another person like him. He goes forward unapologetically into the world and acts accordingly.

My understanding of Lucas all comes from shared experiences. It's about finding a common ground with him and walking it together. Pulling the toy telephone was the first step on that common ground. It was my gesture of goodwill that said, "I am doing this thing that you love so we can be together. Maybe you can do the same thing with one of my activities too."

And that's what happened. Years later, there have been countless times when Lucas has come out for a family event, sisterly performances, or dad-centric day. His agreeable behavior during those times can all be attributed to that opening telephone-pull moment of our relationship. We do for him as he does for us.

CHAPTER 17
Calm Amid the Chaos
Dealing with Sensory Overload

All that said, my son does have moments I can't relate fully to. During those times, it's not about being able to empathize because I "get it." It's about being able to empathize because I love him and I feel for the struggle he's facing.

I'm talking about sensory meltdowns. These are different from tantrums or frustrations about being misunderstood. They are the meltdowns that can feel as though they've come from nowhere and can be impossible to solve. They don't involve giving him a cookie or a device. They're just the outpouring of emotions in a way that leave my boy breathless.

For many kids, these can happen because sensory input—be it too much noise, light, or a deviation from an expected routine—can be too intense for a child with autism to process. He could be walking along smiling, and then suddenly he's not.

Whether he drops to the floor or just breaks into tears, these reactions might seem random, but they're not. Whatever the issue, it's one that's real to him. He's feeling something that I don't understand or see. I don't know the motive. I just know he needs help. That's what I'm there for.

Handling these meltdowns requires patience, understanding, and a calm demeanor. My attitude needs to mirror the attitude that I want him to show. Getting upset or freaking out in response only makes things worse.

Not only would it make things worse in the short term, as he will definitely cry more and become more upset, but it also negatively impacts us in the long term. Over time, he'll know he can't count on me in times like these. For a non-verbal boy who learns mostly from repetition and life experiences, showing him that would be detrimental to our relationship.

Of course, none of that matters because instinct alone tells me not to do that. As a dad, I'm looking down at my son sobbing and rolling on the ground in a fit of distress. Maybe it's the heart meds or maybe it's me, but my inner voice doesn't tell me to get upset in those moments. It tells me to be compassionate. It tells me to be a parent.

My approach is simple yet rooted deeply in being the same calming presence that I remember wishing for as a child. I stay close, offer physical reassurance like back rubs, and maintain a soothing tone. This method doesn't always quiet the meltdown immediately, but it communicates safety and love. I repeat "shhhh" in a soft voice.

That's all it takes. Is it always convenient? No. As I said, this isn't on a timed schedule. He could suddenly become upset out of nowhere. That means it can occur in a crowded store, going down a flight of stairs, or walking through a parking lot teeming with cars. A lot could be going on.

I've sat down next to him on gravel, on a pavement, and in the pouring rain. When his senses get sent into a tailspin, it's not about keeping my pants clean; it's about getting him to a place where he feels calm and safe. That's so much of what being a parent to a non-verbal child is all about.

While hard to telegraph an incoming meltdown, transitions are always an easy place to start. For many kids on the spectrum, moving from one place or activity can often produce a sense of anxiety. Whether it's walking the hallways at school, getting on and off the school bus, or simply going to bed, the time for change can easily be the time for tears.

For a solid year, we dealt with this at school. For some reason, Lucas would lose his mind when he came walking down the hallway at school and saw me there to pick him up. It was mortifying, and I had no idea why.

I'd be waiting, all excited, and ready to collect him from his long day. As soon as he'd turn the corner, I'd clap and give him a big smile. That's when my little buddy would see me… and lose his mind.

Seriously. I had no idea what the hell was happening. Screaming, swatting at the teacher aides around him, and dropping to the floor, Lucas acted like he was about to be thrown off a building. It took at least 10 minutes each time to get him to simply walk off with me. I peeled this kid off the ground every day as kindergartners walked around his limp body.

It was so bad that I could feel the stares from other parents... who all had special needs kids too. That's always a bad sign. These were our people and even they were like, "What the eff is up with this dad?"

Within seconds of walking away from the school and firmly out of earshot, Lucas was beaming with happiness, laughing, and pulling me over for a kiss. It was maddening. I would look back to see if his teachers saw, but they usually had gone back inside by then.

"You're killing me, buddy. They probably think I molest you."

Why did he do this? No idea. I also have no idea why he suddenly stopped doing it one day. Lucas does what Lucas does. We just hold on for the ride.

At the end of the day, everything is manageable when you remember that a child like mine is still a child. He's not here to make life difficult. If anything, he yearns for a peaceful life, just as I do. Moments like this aren't done to break the peace; they're done because Lucas can't handle whatever he's feeling and doesn't know why.

There's always a reason behind a meltdown, even if it's not immediately apparent. By being present and responsive, I aim not only to manage the situation, but also to understand it, showing my son that he's never alone in his challenges.

That's what it means to be a parent for any child. Give them a sense of security and love. If more of us did that, perhaps there would be fewer angry adults walking around today. Be the change you want to see in the world. Teach your kids to do the same. Then send them into the world to be the best they can be.

CHAPTER 18

Her Brother, Not Her Burden

Supporting Supportive Siblings

When I talk about the lessons I strive to teach Lucas, it's important to highlight that I've been equally dedicated to instilling those same values in my daughter, Olivia. Being three years older than her brother, Olivia has grown into the perfect sibling I always hoped she'd be for him.

It was crucial to me that Olivia never felt responsible for Lucas. I wanted him to be her brother, not her burden. Especially when they were younger, I made it a point to ensure she was never put in a position where she had to prevent his impulsive actions or take the blame for his behavior.

It would've been easy to slip into that mindset. Picture coming home to find the living room destroyed after leaving your older daughter with her non-verbal brother. The instinct to flip out is real—I know it well. My urge to lose it surfaces regularly, even as an adult.

But so does my ability to control that impulse. I might say something like, "Did you just watch him rip the door off the hinges?" But during those early days of nurturing their relationship, I kept comments like that to a minimum. Sure, she needed to be reminded to keep him safe, but ultimately watching over Lucas was tough for an adult, much less an elementary school-aged kid less than three years older.

This approach fostered a bond between them that I sometimes forget is even there. As Lucas grew older, I often found myself hovering over him. I've been called a "helicopter parent" more than once, a label I've never appreciated. Yes, Karen, I am a helicopter parent—but that's because my kid is navigating a crowded city without a license. I'm just trying to prevent a disaster.

With Olivia, though, I don't need to hover. When they were younger, she would often lead me out of the room and into the hallway so she and Lucas could read stories together. More than once, I found myself standing there with a dumb smile on my face as the door gently slammed in front of me.

That bond between them has only grown stronger over the years. Olivia has always had a natural instinct to protect her brother, even without being asked. It's something I've witnessed countless times, but one moment stands out.

When your child is non-verbal with autism, you rely heavily on his teachers to fill in the gaps about his day. For

Lucas, his daily communication book has been our lifeline, helping us bridge the classroom and home. But sometimes those notes reveal more than just academic progress.

One day, when he was about seven, after reading through the usual updates, I came across a note that caught my attention:

> Also, I just wanted to mention that another student pinched Lucas's arm at lunch. He didn't seem bothered, but we sent him to the nurse so she could put some ice on it just in case.

I immediately checked him over, looking for any signs of injury. I rubbed his arms, asking if he was hurt, though I knew a response wasn't guaranteed. My boy didn't express pain outside of the moment that it happened. Asking him about an issue that came up yesterday was completely futile. Within minutes, he's over it.

Lucas seemed completely unfazed, and with no visible marks, I wasn't overly concerned. I told myself it was probably just one of those things. Kids being kids.

Still, as I packed his backpack the next morning, the thought lingered. Was this pincher a boy in his special education class or some random kid at lunch? That makes a difference. It poked at my brain, and as Olivia was tying her shoes on the couch in my office, I casually mentioned the incident.

"Lucas's teacher says a kid pinched him at lunch. I wrote

to her to see if it was a student in his class or someone from another class. If it's a stranger kid, that's not good."

Olivia froze mid-tie, her head snapping up. With a seriousness that caught me off guard, she asked, "Wait a minute. This kid has autism?"

"I'm not sure," I replied. "That's why I wrote to his teacher. I think so."

Her next words left me both surprised and incredibly proud.

"He better have autism, or else he's dead meat."

I couldn't help but smile at the fierceness in her voice and the way she hit her fist into her palm. It wasn't something I had ever explicitly taught her. This protective instinct was just part of who she was. No one was going to hurt her brother if she had anything to say about it.

I gave her a hug, reassured by the fact that Lucas had someone like Olivia in his corner. And as I waited for him to return home, eager to hear more from his teacher, I realized that the world might be a challenging place, but with a sister like Olivia, Lucas would always have someone watching his back.

Before the day ended, his teacher called to clarify what had happened. It turned out that the pinch came from a classmate who wanted something Lucas was eating. The situation had been handled, with the other child being removed until he could control his impulses better. As the parent to a little food gobbler myself, I was understanding.

Creating bonds like that requires more than a laid-back approach to babysitting. As a dad, it takes observation and understanding. I've tried to make that a part of our daily lives together.

As children get older, the morning bells for school get progressively earlier. It gets even more annoying when my children, only about three years apart, have such vastly different start times. Lucas was still heading in close to nine, while his sister, who had just entered high school, was starting her day with the farmers.

I don't know if they make these kids toil the soil or what, but it's pretty insane. How do you learn anything that early in the morning? I routinely forget to put a cup under the Keurig coffee maker at that time and flood the kitchen with dark roast. She's expected to do algebra.

Despite his late start, my son gets up ridiculously early too. He is usually up before she is, banging on the gate and waking me up. This was one such morning.

Still, Dad persevered. I got Lucas dressed, fed them both, and prepared to take off. As I did, I tried to snap a picture of the two of them together. As they've grown, I have a million of him and, like, three of her. I rarely ask, and this was one of those times. I tried to pose them. It didn't go well.

At the time, my daughter was rebelling against photographs.

She'd either scowl, stick out her tongue, or complain about being late to wherever we need to go. She did all three this time, and that's when the camel's back buckled under the straw.

"Alright. Enough. Get in the car! Everyone! All I ask is one picture! Just one! Ugh!"

Keep in mind, I almost never raise my voice, so this was a major and very unnecessary moment. I'm not sure what set me off, but sometimes my inner psycho comes out to play in the most unexpected times.

"Damnit!"

See?

They both walked towards the car, and as my daughter was getting in, Lucas brushed past her. He banged into her door, sending it flying into her head. I watched as her noggin bounced off the car's frame before she slunk into the seat. It looked brutal.

From the front of the car, I knocked on the hood. She made eye contact, and I used my awesome non-verbal communication skills. Pointing to my head and frowning, I mouthed, "Are you okay?"

Her response was the ol' "whatever" shrug she does. That was the cue that it was fine.

But really, it wasn't. I could tell she was in pain, and as we drove, I asked her, and she verified it. I felt terrible for her, mainly because it happened right after my fatherly meltdown. Yet there was something else to all this. Something that overshadowed everything.

I was incredibly proud of her.

Think about it. Her brother just slammed a freakin' car door into her head with force. There was no meaningful apology afterward, as he doesn't have the vocabulary or understanding to express it. In fact, this response could be misinterpreted as jubilation to those who don't know him—Lucas just hopped into the car and began playing on his electronic device while she rubbed her skull and stared out the window.

In that moment, though, it wasn't about what she did. It was about what she *didn't* do. She didn't yell. She didn't scream. She didn't curse at him or complain that he gets away with everything. She understood the reality of our situation, and she forgave him. There was no anger or resentment. She was an amazing sister.

It's something that most people reading this might think, "Of course not, it's not his fault. How could she blame him?" Well, that's easier said than done. We all like to think that's how you handle the situation, but as someone who has been in this exact situation countless times with Lucas, I know that it's not easy to stay so level-headed, especially when he just leveled your head with the passenger door.

After dropping them both off at school, I went to Kohl's and walked straight to the jewelry section. Almost immediately, I stumbled onto a bracelet engraved with the word "Sister." I purchased it right away.

Once school was over, I told her how proud I was of how she had handled the issue.

"Yeah, but you got mad at me," she said.

"Yeah, before the head thing. I got mad because you purposely make miserable faces in pictures. That's weird and I'm still mad about that. This isn't that."

I reminded her that her brother loved her and would never hurt her on purpose. When we got home, I explained he had a present he wanted to give her.

Once the gang was all reunited in the kitchen, I had Lucas walk it over and hand her the box. She was so happy when she opened it, and has worn it since she received it.

The next day, when Lucas kept insisting on more Pirate's Booty cereal, I felt my annoyance creeping up, and after about ten refusals and him tugging my arm to stand up, I said, "Lucas...no!" That's when Olivia chimed in.

"Hey. No getting mad at Lucas."

And she was right.

The relationship my kids have is the relationship I always wanted for them. It's something I feared would be impossible when Lucas's special needs began to emerge. I never wanted Olivia to view him as a burden or a responsibility. Her brother isn't a chore. He's her family for life. He loves her and looks up to her in all the ways he knows how to.

What made that possible is moments like this one. It was buying her birthday gifts from him and having her help with his bedtimes. There were matching pajamas during the holidays and lazy afternoons running around the basement. She never had an autistic brother; she had a brother with autism. Just like son, friend, and other identifiers, the fact that he is her sibling comes before anything else.

CHAPTER 19

Feeling Alone While You're Surrounded

Finding Your Tribe

My son's dignity is important to me. One of the main concerns I had with raising a boy like Lucas in the early years was the reaction from the public. I thought deeply about how strangers would act when we were out and he was acting difficult.

Keep in mind, I'm not talking about their perception of him or how they might view him. That doesn't make a difference to me. I know that there are strangers judging other people constantly. Regardless of who my son was, there would be a person across a Target store secretly thinking something. For some, that's the way they live.

The issue that scared me was how I would handle it if someone actually gawked, approached, or said something. I had read horror stories online about old women coming up to stressed-out parents in the produce section of a supermarket and remarking about their kid's needs to be "straightened out."

I couldn't even imagine. As a person who had long created mental scenarios where I fought the entire town like a scene in a kung fu movie, I couldn't fathom what I would do. The images played out like a movie in my head.

"Excuse me, but that little boy needs some discipline. Why is he clapping and screaming like that?"

"You have insulted my honor. Prepare to get trashed in the vegetable section."

Headband. Karate stance. Spin kick. People flying backwards. Lettuce shooting through the air. You can see it. Maybe a giant deli worker comes from the back with a meat cleaver. I told you. I really get into these things.

Trust me, I was ready. If anyone had anything to say, I was all set to take them down.

Do you know how many confrontational situations with strangers about Lucas have played out in our lifetime? Zero.

Have there been elderly waitresses who disregarded us and I knew it was because of him? Sure. Have people looked over when he yelled? Absolutely, but that's understandable. Never, though, has anyone come up to me with an insulting comment.

My paranoia, however, has played tricks on me and taught

me important lessons about those around us. The world that I feared would be so cruel to my child has been surprisingly kind. My brain still tells me that it is a trick from time to time, though.

There was a Father's Day a few years ago when our entire family went to a typical Long Island seaside restaurant. Lucas was still small and his iPad, a luxury I often leave in the car during outings like this today, was in his hand. It still had a calming effect during those years, as opposed to revving him up like a Roman candle today. So he was well behaved as he swiped away on that Sunday.

We were seated inside, right beside a giant glass window. The sun was overhead and we were all content. Diners were seated on the other side of the glass, enjoying their own meals on the deck. I barely noticed them.

Then, as we were ordering, I could see a family from the corner of my eye. Their son was nine or ten years old and was looking through the window at us. The image was hazy as I didn't want to make eye contact. My concern was Lucas and making sure he was well behaved.

And he was. My little man was on his best behavior, which, at that time, said a lot. Keeping him both calm and patient for food was a tough task, but he was pulling through with flying colors. I couldn't have been prouder.

From over his shoulder, through the window, I could see this older boy seated at an outdoor table with his family. It was my peripheral vision, but I could clearly make out that he was jumping around in his seat and seemingly entertaining his mom and dad. While they were in my vision, they weren't my focus.

As the meal went on, I noticed the boy peering through the window at my son's iPad. Again, it was just from the corner of my eye, so I didn't get a clear view, but I could see it happening. My dad senses spiked, but ultimately I ignored it and figured it was just what kids do. They're curious. There was nothing wrong with that, and as long as no one bothered us, I wasn't bothered. We were fine.

Lucas, I want to add, was still being an angel. The meal took forever to come out, but he displayed so much maturity during the wait. While my eyes were planted on my boy and his impeccable behavior, though, I still had a hazy view of the people behind him.

That's where I saw...and was almost positive that the boy was not only looking at him, but laughing, as he turned back to his family.

What the hell?

My daddy anger senses started to bubble up inside. Lucas doesn't register ridicule or mockery, but I do. I'm his protector and I was not happy about it. So this time, I looked up and made my vision noticeable. I stared darts through the glass to see this kid quickly turn around to peer in our direction, once again with uproarious laughter, and then turn back to his parents.

Then I saw something that made my blood boil. Get this—his parents were laughing too. I was enraged. What should I do? My split-second instinct was to smash the glass and barrel through like the Incredible Hulk. This was it. It's not a drill. This is the ninja spin-kick fighting I had dreamed of. It's on.

Although...I knew that would ruin Father's Day, and probably my life, all for an offensive action that I wasn't sure was even happening. Our minds tell us to react immediately, but being a grown-up tells us to temper our actions with wisdom. And to be honest, I was more confused by all this than angry. Lucas hadn't done anything to raise their interest. Why were they laughing at him?

I continued to glare through the window at this giggly family and was no longer hiding it. I hated how this carefree group was all laughing together at my son for what I can only assume they saw as his differences. What kind of family would do that? I just sat there staring at them.

Their stupid faces were right there in their stupid chairs, giggling, and eating stupid garlic bread. All judgmental as the dad puts his son on his lap and starts tickling him. The stupid...

"Wait. What?"

As I mentioned, this boy was older than my son. Most children don't do that in the middle of restaurants when they are near ten years old. I know my daughter didn't. It didn't seem typical. It seemed like something more in tune with what Lucas would do.

Then, for the first time the whole meal, I really looked at this boy and his family—not from an angry side gaze, but from a direct stare. That's when I saw it. This kid wasn't making fun of Lucas.

He was just like Lucas.

I don't simply mean that he appeared to have special needs, although he did, but he also shadowed my son's mannerisms and behavior more than anyone I had ever seen. I watched as the boy hopped around, laughed wildly, while his parents took turns bopping him up and down on their laps. I noticed his darting glances, casual shouts, and, for the first time, I saw his iPad.

It was the same as the one my son has—complete with a matching carrying case.

That's what they had been looking at. That's why they had been laughing. The stares, laughs, and seemingly rude behavior was all just their reaction to seeing something they thought was *similar* about us, not different. I never saw it coming.

I've thought a lot about that day. I've gone over my false assumptions about strangers. I imagined the worst in people and assumed it all was happening around me.

Yet, when I stopped imagining and focused, both figuratively and literally, on the people who really were around us, I saw that it wasn't about our differences. I saw that these people were much more like us than I could have ever thought. From the corner of my eye, I didn't see it. I had to look directly to see them for who they are. If I never had, then my memory of that day would have been much different than the reality it truly was.

Poetic, right? It sounds like something you read in English class and then do a report on. Yet, it happened in real life. The symbolism was shockingly on point. It was as if someone was writing this out for me to read, rather than to live.

This was a much-needed reminder that while autism is unique and special needs are special, they still exist outside our home. It can be easy to feel alone when in a family like ours, but that's not always the true story. It's the voice in our heads stoking the flames of our worst fears.

This boy and his family showed me that we weren't as alone in the world as I felt. There are plenty of people just like me and my son. Sure, the differences can be overwhelming at first glance, but once you focus on who people truly are rather than hazy assumptions from the corner of your eye, you'll see many more similarities than you ever did before. I know I did.

Trying to remember that keeps me grounded and less defensive. It gives me the chance to deal with Lucas's struggles publicly without worrying about the staring eyes around us. That's why I'm able to calm him during his toughest times and give outsiders a glimpse of the best Lucas has to offer.

HI WORLD, I'M DAD

Because of that, there have been times when people have approached me with positive feedback. In one of my most cherished moments from fatherhood, Lucas was melting down at our local pool. I needed to get him out and he was having none of it.

Screaming, splashing, and carrying on, my not-so-little fella was not leaving this water when it was time to go, and I envisioned having to call the coast guard to send a helicopter. During times of extreme moods, it's sometimes difficult to see any light at the end of the tunnel. All you're thinking is that this will never end.

The biggest issue is that you can't just give in. Sure, I could have let him stay and swim some more, but we needed to leave to get his sister from school, and I had already expressed that to him. Remaining in the water would just solidify the fact that tantrums get you what you want.

When this happens, I don't fight him. I try to speak calmly and rub his back. It seems so out of the ordinary as most parents would be screaming, or at the very least, dragging him out. However, I learned long ago that this wasn't the way to get things done.

That lesson came to me from Nintendo®. As a kid, I'd spend 10 minutes trying to beat a level on *Mario Bros.* only to be left frustrated. To get my insane aggression out, I would take the controller, spin it around like a lasso, and slam it into the wall. What was the result? I now still had to beat the level...with a controller that made a clicking noise and didn't go left. Angry explosions do nothing but make the task harder to finish.

In times like these, I remembered that. Lucas is my boy and I know that freaking out on him doesn't help. It makes him freak out more in return. Calm begets calm with my guy. So I offer calm. I show him patience.

That's what I was doing at the pool as his energy level started to flutter down. Lucas went from yelling to breathing to ready to leave. I knew I had accomplished my goal and prepared to exit the pool.

That's when an older man who had been swimming came wading over and tapped me on the shoulder. Visions of produce-section karate battles danced through my head. I turned to him, ready for anything he was about to say. That's when he said the one thing I wasn't prepared for.

"Excuse me. I just needed to come over and tell you that you're a wonderful father."

I'm not a big crier, but I wanted to burst into tears. Even now, writing this, I feel such a sense of pride and joy in that compliment. There was nothing he could have said that would have topped that. It touched my heart on so many levels.

Obviously, I loved the fact that I was seen as a good father to Lucas. All I want is to do right by my boy. Knowing that even in my harshest of moments someone can see my actions from afar and acknowledge that I'm doing the right thing fills me with a sense of fatherly gratitude.

For that man, we were an example of autism in the community and how it is best handled. It was someone who may have been aware of autism or even accepted it. My goal, however, was to make sure he and others could appreciate it.

Words that we ourselves say and how we say them play a huge role in the community. The fact that wording is such an important part of having a non-verbal child feels like the very definition of irony.

There are little things. The word "autistic" is one of them. I don't use it. By the same token, I'm not offended by it. It's just not what I personally do.

Rather, I say my son is "my child with autism." In my mind, Lucas is my child first and his autism comes second. Just like my daughter is my child who plays tennis. It's a personal choice that I made personally.

I don't care what other people say or do. That's up to them. Yet, you'll find people bogged down in details and battling one another over it. I've seen comments on social media under a post or two that responds to me saying "with autism." It will simply say, "You mean autistic."

No, Karen. I don't. You're muddying the water. Let's just be a community.

To each his own. Live and let live. Smoke 'em, if you got 'em. Whatever. Life's too short for silliness.

CHAPTER 20
Autism Awareness
For a Family and for Society

The bigger debate is awareness versus acceptance. Find someone who supports autism acceptance and they'll make it sound like saying "autism awareness" is the same as throwing eggs at a person. In reality, they're both different things. They play different roles within the community and for people in general.

Autism awareness and autism acceptance both represent positives for people like my son and others on the spectrum. Yet, as someone who has experienced both, I feel that autism appreciation is the big one that people need to be more aware of.

Yes, yes. Now there's a third one. Please, bear with me. I'm not throwing a third party candidate into the mix. In fact, appreciation is based on the other two; it has a different place among both families affected by autism and those within society in general. Allow me to explain.

Autism awareness for a family affected by autism

For me, personally, autism awareness was the toughest of the three. I had to become aware that my son had autism. I had to realize that what I was seeing were truly signs that he was on the spectrum.

Lucas's actions may be unique, but there were "red flags" that were straight from a 90s health class video. His clapping, wobbly walking, and hand flapping at an early age all sent shivers down my spine to witness. I worried constantly.

Saying that now, as the father of a non-verbal teenage boy, is painful. I hate to admit that I worried about Lucas growing up to have autism because, well, he did. Now that he's here, I wouldn't trade him for the world. But back then, I didn't know that yet.

There was no way to see what our relationship would be like today when I worried back then. When I feel guilt now, looking back, I remind myself of that. There's no shame in worrying your child could have delays, special needs, or long-term disabilities. Rather, it would be weird if you didn't.

"What's that, doc? Autism? Oh. Okay. Sounds good. Do you know if there's a Taco Bell around here?"

My brain was constantly worried about Lucas when he was little. I saw all the signs and felt completely alone. I didn't want to think it, and I especially didn't want to say it out loud. A part of me felt like the world could see it.

Once, a relative remarked on his hand flapping as if it was "cute." At a time when my mind was beating me up from the inside out, she actually turned to me and said:

"Aw, look at him. His little hand flaps. I love it."

I wanted to scream, "What is wrong with you!? How could you say that?!" Of course, you can't. That would be saying the quiet part out loud. If I ever said the word "autism," then it would come true. That was my thinking at the time. That's what I tortured myself with. That's why I fought through that music class for years.

Then, one day, I said it out loud.

We were at the California Pizza Kitchen, having a big dinner with extended family. Lucas was rocking back and forth in his booster seat. As he did, he'd bang his chest into the table without a care in the world. People were smiling and laughing. One chuckling family member said, "Be careful, Lucas. What are you doing? Are you okay?"

To this, I said, "I don't think he's okay. I think something's wrong."

I don't know why I said it, and I remember regretting it immediately. The reactions were not good, and it was as if I just set the menus on fire. Needless to say, it wasn't a great meal at the ol' CPK, and an even less fun ride home.

That was the day that I and the rest of the people around us became aware that my son had autism. That was how we found our personal "autism awareness."

Oh boy, were we ever all aware after that.

Autism awareness for society

For society in general, autism awareness is a bit different. It lets others know that people like Lucas are out there. His noises and behavior in public aren't for fun or something to be stared at; it's part of who he is.

While I definitely understand how families can condemn awareness as not being "enough" for their loved ones to find a place in society, it's actually been valuable to a family like mine.

Lucas has what some would call "severe autism." Again, it's a game of semantics, with many debating the right term to use. Whatever you want to call it, I don't care. He has it.

My boy will never have to "come out" to his friends as having autism one day. Barring any major change, he will need assistance for the rest of his life, and that's just how it is.

I want the world to be aware of my son. People need to see him and understand that the things he does aren't to cause a commotion or be gawked at. Lucas lives as Lucas lives. I will do my best to make sure he doesn't infringe on others, and I want them to do the same for him.

AUTISM AWARENESS

This is an important thing for me because, as I've said many times, I felt that having a child like Lucas would mean that I would have to have many street fights.

I'm from New York. People around here can sometimes be a little blunt and it extends beyond, "Hey! I'm walking here!" Many of us walk around worrying that someone is going to say something that requires an attitude adjustment.

To go into the world with a person who claps and screeches during times of excitement can feel like you're guiding Daniel into the lion's den. My initial concerns were that I would need to field many rude glares.

I haven't. Maybe it's because I haven't looked around enough, but either way, I have barely seen any of those stares that I dreaded when he was little. Over the course of the last decade, my son's outbursts, especially when they're not overwhelming, draw little attention. It's far less of a problem than I ever dreamed.

For that, I credit autism awareness. The work that schools, media, and organizations do to drive an understanding that people like Lucas live life differently has been so instrumental in easing any concerns I might have. It's also done wonderful work in helping others see that the person he is may appear different, but there's a beautiful reason for it. This is who he is. We just wanted you to be aware.

CHAPTER 21

Autism Acceptance

For a Family and for Society

Autism acceptance for a family affected by autism

When it came to having autism in our lives, I wasn't against the idea per se. Sure, that drive home from the restaurant framed it all in a terrible light, and the team of experts that followed did nothing to ease those concerns.

We were certainly aware that something was wrong, but hoped against hope that it was something else. No matter who we spoke to at this time, there were tons of "hopeful" pieces of advice.

Whether it's stories of neighbors with grandkids who didn't speak until they were 12 or friends of friends with kids misdiagnosed, everyone was busy trying to steer us in a more positive direction. Of course, to many, positive meant speech.

They said it directly. The most said quote was, "Don't worry. It'll be fine. He'll talk eventually."

Well, sorry to say, that never happened. My son still hasn't spoken a verbal word. It begs the question—does that mean he isn't "fine"?

Spoiler alert, he's more than fine. He's perfect. Still, the implication was that without language, he'd be flawed. It made the eventual acceptance even harder to stomach for a dad who was already beating the hell out of himself behind closed doors.

What a selfish person I was. How could I bring this boy into the world and hand him a lifetime of sorrow? I wasn't exaggerating either. "Autism" had long been viewed as a bad word. Watch out when you raise your kids or else they'll catch "the autism."

And here I am, with a kid showing all the signs of autism. Every possible exit route was more than welcome and there were plenty of them along the way. People can't wait to give you that out.

While the ol' "maybe he'll come around" assurance sounds dismissive, it's a piece of hope that any terrified parent clings to. I know I did. Still, there were other possibilities looming.

When you combine that fatherly guilt with the team of people hoping to help me out of my dark mental place, it can create some pretty huge false hopes. That's what led me to an excited thought that I never would have dreamed would be an excited thought.

Maybe he's deaf! Yay!

I kid you not. I was jumping for joy in hopes that my son couldn't hear. If that was the case, it would explain everything. That's why he didn't look up when people entered a room. It's why he couldn't imitate language or join in with fun activities. It's all in the ears!

To prove this to myself, I'd sit behind him as he played on the floor and whisper his name.

"Lucasssss... Lucasssss..."

Yeah, it was as creepy as it sounds. When he wouldn't react to hearing me call him, I'd celebrate this piece of sure-fire proof. When he did respond, I told myself it was just a coincidence. Yeah, Denial—party of one. Your table is served.

That table was set at a hospital out on Long Island that I happily drove my son to in order to have his hearing checked. The ride there was spent with my yelling to him in the backseat.

"Buddy! I don't know if you can hear me, but we're gonna find out! You ready!? We're going to get you fixed up!"

Still a toddler, Lucas was seated on my lap as the doctor ran some hearing tests. I was intrigued by the setup and tried to understand how they'd know. She assured me that she would, and explained in a way that I should have understood, but I was too excited to respond.

My brain was already in another place. I was picturing cochlear implants on my son, on stage as an adult, signing to an audience that his book about hearing loss was dedicated to his dad. Futuristic people were on their feet cheering for us. Confetti would fall from the sky. Tears streaming down the faces of all the...

"Okay, Mr. Guttman, he doesn't have any hearing problems. This could mean..."

I hadn't even noticed that the test was over, and with it, my hopes for an alternative to autism. The doctor's voice echoed and a loud droning siren played out over her final explanations. I had nothing left to hear anyway. That was it. I had made my last play. My son can hear. He has autism.

I accepted it.

Autism acceptance for society

If it sounds like I wasn't enthused with having to accept autism in my life, you're right. I always felt that the autism acceptance movement has a similar feel.

Accepting something doesn't sound joyful to me. It sounds

like something a judge gives an attorney with a warning: "I'll accept it, McGinty, but watch your line of questioning."

To me, acceptance should be part of awareness. What kind of jerk is aware of something and doesn't accept it? This isn't Santa Claus, grandma. This is a real person in front of you. If you know my son exists, who are you to not allow him into your world?

You better accept him! That's acceptance to me. It feels like we're forcing outsiders to take in people like my son as if it's some big ask. In reality, my son is amazing and these shnooks are lucky to know him. Lucas should be made to accept them, not the other way around.

Now, all that being said, I would be self-centered to not see a spectrum that extends beyond my son. I think so often the autism community gets mired down in their own personal relationship with autism that they discount the struggles of others.

Low functioning vs. high functioning—it feels ridiculous. Anyone who has ever been marginalized by society should stand in solidarity with others in that situation. That's what I do. Just because my son doesn't deal with issues associated with those on a higher level of understanding doesn't mean I discount their struggles.

I said earlier that Lucas will never have to "come out" as having autism. The prospects for love and employment are so far off in the future, if at all, that they would most likely never be an issue in his life. The people who have to accept him don't have to accept him and he still wouldn't care. Just give him some Pirate's Booty cereal and his iPad and he'll just clap you off into the air.

There are, however, people who will have to come out as having autism. They'll function at a level that allows them to seek out social and romantic relationships. They'll need to find jobs and careers to keep their lights on. They'll have to do all of these things while handling the issues that those on the spectrum have to handle, whatever that might mean for them individually.

For those people, autism acceptance is so important. My heart goes out to anyone who has to handle some of these things, and even though my family doesn't deal with that type of autism, that doesn't make the struggle any less real.

As an advocate for autism, I support all people with autism. Whether you're non-verbal like my son or otherwise, there's no reason that people on the spectrum should have to ask for acceptance. It should just be something we all do.

To be honest, if you met someone like my son or some of the other people in the community I have been blessed to meet through the years, you'd know how fortunate you are to have them in your life. There's something unique and beautiful about autism in many ways. That's what autism appreciation is.

CHAPTER 22
Autism Appreciation
For a Family and for Society

I wish it hadn't taken a near-death experience to make me realize how lucky I was to have a child like mine.

That's not to say that I didn't know I had a great kid. I did. Lucas, though, was still small. Not even two, my little guy was still technically a baby. His personality hadn't come out yet. I didn't know who he was or who he would be.

All I knew was that something was "wrong." I say that because that's how autism was always framed. No one ever talked about a child potentially having autism as anything other than a major tragedy.

So, when my child had autism, that's exactly what it felt like. It was a tragic moment for our family. The world was crashing. The sky was falling, The worst part?

I didn't even know what that meant. No one could define what exactly this was. What was autism? How would it affect my son? What would be the end result once he aged out of this early childhood era? There was nothing more than a shrug, a warning, and a sense of impending doom.

That impending doom never came to pass, at least not in the ways I expected. It's that realization that changed my life in so many ways. It was that realization that set me on an easier path.

I felt silly. I felt like I had spent too long looking into a future without having all proper context there to help me along. The world I envisioned with a non-verbal child was a world with a stranger. I was projecting this baby in my living room into adulthood. I pictured being tasked with helping him live his daily life without even knowing who he is. All I could see was the burden.

Living my life in real time, I can tell you that the imagined scenario was dark and hazy while the real life scenario is simple. My son, who I love with all my heart, is the person I am tasked with helping through life. It's easy because I love him.

Make no mistake, I don't just love him because he's mine. This isn't the case of just shrugging and saying, "You get what you get, Pinkalicious." No. This is reality. Over the last decade, I've come to know, understand, and appreciate my boy.

Autism appreciation is different than accepting who he is. It's light years beyond simply being aware that he's here.

Autism appreciation is about acknowledging the beautiful aspects of Lucas's personality because of, not despite, autism.

My son has no ego. He's not brash or conceited. When Lucas gives you a hug, it's because he wants to hug you. It's not to get something or sweeten you up for a selfish act. He's completely himself in every way.

You've read a laundry list of things about him throughout this book and shared in my joy of being his father. You've also seen that—yes—autism does create some unique challenges in our lives. It also, although rarely pointed out, eliminates some too.

In all probability my son won't experience heartbreak the way many of us do. He doesn't, as of today, understand loss or grief. There's no cyberbullying. In fact, there's no bullying at all. If someone is mean to my boy, he doesn't get it. He just goes about his day and lets it roll off his shoulders like we all wish we could.

It's his dad who comes flying out with a spin kick. I'm just waiting, hyah!

Lucas Guttman is the realist person I've ever met and the purest soul I've ever known. Unlike others who may present that way, only to reveal their true nature during times of struggle, he is authentic. He's completely himself and unapologetically so.

And that's because of autism.

And that's why I appreciate it. If my son saw the world any other way, he'd be a different person. That's a major thing. It also helps to eliminate any desire I may have had to see him "cured" of autism.

Do I want to see him learn all the life skills he doesn't have? Yes. I'd love to wake up and hear my boy singing as he happily brushes his hair for school. That would be amazing.

I wouldn't, however, make a wish for him to suddenly not have autism. Lucas without autism would be a different person. He would be someone I don't know, and to be frank, magically hearing him use words isn't worth the trade-off of losing this special person who views the world through such a beautiful lens.

You may have noticed that, unlike acceptance and awareness, autism appreciation doesn't have to be divided up between how it affects a family and the public. That's because it encompasses everyone the same way.

The appreciation we show to people like Lucas goes beyond our walls. It's for everyone to see and experience. The only distinction is that, in order to showcase this for the outside world, families like mine need to put our best foot forward and share the triumphs of our children rather than the pitfalls.

If you were served the best pasta you've ever eaten by the worst waiter you ever had, which part of the story do you lead with? That makes all the difference. We lead with the good aspects without pretending the negatives don't exist.

AUTISM APPRECIATION

The best parts of Lucas are the parts that people don't know about. Those are the parts we share first.

Doing that opens the door for everyone to see the beauty in my son. People are conditioned to stay away and wait for an invitation to interact with him. Showing his best side and explaining why he's so special invites people in. It shows them that autism isn't something to be feared; it's something to be appreciated.

Once they do that, then awareness and acceptance just come along for the ride. They're a package deal.

I love someone with autism. I want the world to love him too. By remembering that, we're doing our part—not only for Lucas, but for everyone on the spectrum.

So, you've had a chance to read my thoughts and understand our family. I've demonstrated our reality and provided an insight into what makes my boy's challenges more than something for us to simply handle. They're the building blocks of his unique and wonderful personality. For those who know us, the reasons for autism appreciation are obvious.

I do know, however, that there are still some out there who think this is all feel-goodery nonsense. They question my true feelings and will probably mutter something about doing it to sell books.

Before anything, autism appreciation has been a concept I have been pushing for years, long before a book was even a consideration. My blog has always been free of any personal ads or sponsored content. Even our podcast has no commercials or advertisements. This isn't to sell books. It isn't to sell anything—including Lucas. It's something I believe in and something I feel anyone can see if they truly look at who my son is.

Of course, despite writing for a noble reason, I am aware that I am writing about another human being who might not be able to actually sign off on the content I'm sharing. Because of that, I follow certain rules when telling tales about my boy.

I never narrate him like a puppet. There have been blogs like that too, and it always makes me cringe. I don't know what he's truly thinking and to put my own scripted words into his mouth feels like an obviously awful thing to do. I can guess what his responses are because he's my kid, but I would never craft a dialogue based on creativity and intuition. He deserves more respect than that.

Another promise I made myself when starting these posts was to respect Lucas's privacy. Certain topics are off-limits. I don't go into detail on his deficits of certain life skills like toilet use. Despite questions from readers, I always considered those things to be private. I know that would be something that my son would never want me to tell the world about. None of us would. While I don't like to put words into his mouth, those are words I feel confident in knowing. No one wants their dad to talk about things like that in public.

Does that mean he doesn't use the toilet or handle a variety of basic life skills? I don't know. Maybe he does. Maybe he doesn't. See how easy that is? They can ask, but you don't have to tell. Some things are better left unsaid. Privacy is important. A 13-year-old boy with autism is still a 13-year-old boy. You don't splash his behind-closed-doors news on the front page.

Lucas can't tell his story. People don't know him, and even those who are around him don't get the full experience of his personality. As a writer, I could help show him to everyone and make sure the beauty behind his personality was put on display. Sill, though, this is about my son, and I don't take this task lightly. I want to do him proud, and even if he never understands a single word I wrote, I want to think he would be happy with it, if he could. That's why it's so important to put myself in his shoes and tell our story as we walk side by side.

It's just as important to me to follow these rules as it is to show the world how wonderful my son is. I do, however, get where some of the muttering non-believers are coming from. I know because I was one of them at one time.

Earlier, I said that there was once a time when I wasn't a parent to a non-verbal child with autism. I know what many people think about parents in my situation and the points of view I have expressed here.

There are many thinking, "This guy is deluding himself. He can't accept the awful truth that his kid has autism and can't talk, so he's trying to tell us how 'great' it is. He doesn't believe that."

I do believe it. I can sit here and draw you a roadmap of all the reasons why, but some people won't get it. The funniest part of that?

The reason why they don't understand autism appreciation is the exact reason why I appreciate his autism.

The cynical way they're seeing my message and their distrust for my authenticity is inherently self-centered. It stands in contrast to how Lucas sees the world and goes against the beauty that I'm trying to showcase here. Their disbelief is my exhibit A.

Simply put, people see the world through the lenses they wear. Lucas does too. His lens is bright, vibrant, loving, and trusting. The lenses worn by so many others are not. If I had to choose one personality to have, I'd go with Lucas's every time. That seems like something to be appreciated, right?

What the self-appointed judge's judges don't get is that Lucas doesn't judge anyone. He is an open book of emotions and motivations. Unlike the person who smiles and nods, only to privately question how "great" my son really is, Lucas wears his pristine heart on his sleeve. There's nothing duplicitous about him.

To put it simply, he's not like most of us, and I love that about him. It's what makes him so perfect.

Lucas treats people with love and care. The first time he meets someone, he's always sweet to them right from the start. He'll run over to tap them (a motion of endearment) or offer a clap. Everyone gets fair treatment right from the beginning.

Newcomers to our lives can't believe it. They think it's unique and almost always remark about how he hugged them or had them rub his head. They believe that he must have felt they were special in order to be so welcoming.

They are partially right. He does think they are special, but only because he sees all newcomers as special. Lucas treats you well until you give him a reason not to.

Even then, he still treats people well. Lucas is the opposite of a hater. How's that for something to appreciate?

If you think appreciation is a difficult concept to wrap your head around, how about acceptance? People want others to be accepting. Well, Lucas is the most accepting person I've ever met. Everyone's welcome in his orbit and given a chance to know him. He has autism acceptance in that his autism gives him a sense of acceptance that we all want our kids to demonstrate. Mine does. It's just another thing worth appreciating.

Do you see where I am going with this? The very reason I appreciate my son is that he's not the person to exclude others or harbor ill intentions behind their back. Skills aside, in his heart and as a person, he has all the base qualities we value. Most of them were never even taught. They're just within him. He was born that way.

CHAPTER 23

Disability vs. this Ability

It's All in the Perspective

Think about it realistically. Flash back to my stories about seeing my babies for the first time. Ask someone in that position what they'd want their infants to grow up to be. What would they say?

Of course, people can be materialistic, so some might lead with aspirations or career goals. They'll want their kid to be president or a world champion in whatever. However, in almost every case, they will follow up with something deeper.

"But whatever they become, I'll love them. No matter what happens, if you grow up to be a good person, I'll be happy."

You know I'm telling the truth because you can imagine a new parent saying that. You might have even been that as a new parent yourself. I know I did, and luckily, that's what happened with me. It happened with both my kids. With Lucas, it was pretty much on the nose.

It's such a simple concept and one that we know from the moment our kids arrive. We get caught up in phrasing and hopes, but we all know that our kids come first, and for many, nothing can stop you from loving them. Think about this one: when you ask an expectant parent whether they want a boy or girl, what do most people say?

"It doesn't matter. As long as they're healthy."

Well, let me tell you something that most parents already know, although reading it out loud might be jarring. Being healthy doesn't matter either.

Sure, you want them to be healthy, but you don't *need it* to love them. If you're given the gift of a child, you care for them no matter what. Gender, health, and everything else wash away when you hold them in your arms. If there is something outside their control that makes you stop loving or knowing your kids, that's on you. For most of us, it's inconceivable. I'll never stop loving these kids.

This isn't meant to be judgmental or condescending. In fact, I was one of those "as long as they're healthy" people. It sounds so magnanimous when you say it, but it loses its shine when you examine the meaning. It also plays into the doubt that creeps in when someone suggests they might not be "healthy" in whatever sense you define it.

Memories of hearing "autism" for the first time and coming

to grips with the doubts were dark. Even remembering those times now drags me back in my mind. Never before have I ever felt like an island among a community as I did then. I didn't know what was coming next and I feared everything.

Life changed overnight and our circle had become smaller and smaller until it was a dot. No one understood what we were going through, and no one could relate to our evolving homelife.

Friends with babies, who had literally been our contemporaries one week, were out of it the next. Once the first words started rolling in, people all flew away. Isolation mixed with jealousy makes this joyous time period so terrible for those left without answers.

Suddenly old friends were having playdates and teaching their kids knock knock jokes. All the while, I couldn't even provide an answer when someone would ask if my son knew it was his birthday.

In all fairness, though, what kind of stupid question is that? Don't ask parents to non-verbal kids that question.

Regardless, I didn't know the answer anyway. I didn't know anything. There was so much to teach him and so little time. I wasn't sure he'd ever understand anything, and I beat myself up for not understanding what autism even was in our lives.

It left us lost and resentful in ways that we couldn't properly express. What I'm saying is that the guy I was then, dealing with this terrifying and undefined future, never would have understood autism appreciation. It would have felt like trying to put a party hat on for the end of the world.

So I don't judge you for doubting my veracity. I would have. I come from the world of pro wrestling. Everything is a work. Everything is smoke and mirrors. Retired professional wrestler "Stone Cold" taught us all to not trust anyone. I get why people would feel the same way here.

For parents in the early stages of their autism journey, I understand it even more. The years spent blaming myself were some of the hardest times of my life. No matter what the catalyst was, I knew that Lucas didn't ask to be born; I chose to bring him into the world. I selfishly wanted a child. Now, I've given him the hardest road to walk.

Looking back, it sounds silly. At the time, it was the most serious thing in the world. I had no shame for Lucas. I had shame for myself on the deepest level you could imagine. His struggles weren't embarrassing for me; his struggles were *caused* by me. My son was hurting and I did it. I was the worst person in the world. I was convinced that everyone could see that.

Again, that guy—the worst guy in the world—could never understand autism appreciation. Had I read these words back then, I'd be incredulous. Autism appreciation? How could that be a thing? Autism couldn't be appreciated. It was the bogeyman knocking at the door. Anyone appreciating that is trying to sell magic beans.

I've thought about this long and hard and I know what I would do if I had a time machine. I'd go back to that version of me, give him a hug, and ask what autism meant. James, what exactly was going to happen to your boy?

I know what his answer would be. I know his answer because I was him and I can recall all those late nights, lying awake and thinking about it. Autism meant...autism. Nothing more, nothing less. It was special needs, work, and a child who would never know me. It was like failing the biggest test of life and giving your kid the hardest possible future there was.

There could have been more reasons at the time, but I wasn't sure what they were yet. After all, the whole no-hugging thing from *Rain Man* was offputting, but Lucas hugged. He loves being hugged. To this day, I wrap my arms around him and say, "1...2...3... Squeeeeeze." I grip tighter and he laughs with glee as the air escapes his round little body. No, sir, Mr. Hoffman, my kid loves hugs. That one didn't happen.

What else did I know about autism? Endless questions, right? Is that it? Kids with autism ask endless questions. Well, just like the hugging, that's true for many people on the spectrum. It wasn't true for Lucas, though. He doesn't ask anything because he doesn't have verbal language. Sure, he could use his tablet to ask, but that's for getting chicken nuggets and pizza. Yet another box on the autism list that would go unchecked by my little man.

Of course, I could never tell myself that he'd never speak

from the door of my time machine. Had I known he was going to remain non-verbal back then, I would have lost my mind and made that my number one contention of fear. Non-verbal was the end of the world. If that comes true, then that's the worst part.

That's it. Autism was scary because it will rob my son of language. Yeah, that's the ticket. That's what I'm scared of. He'll never be able to communicate with me.

Except, that's not true either. Lucas and I communicate. It goes beyond that food-ordering tablet, as I mentioned. We also have hand gestures and intuition. Being Lucas's dad is like having a friend across the room during a boring meeting all the time. One glance and annoyed face goes a long way, even if your friend doesn't get the exact meaning each time. You flash an expression or hand gesture, and he just knows.

So, yeah. It's yet another misconception that shaped my trembling view of who my boy would be. Even when my non-verbal fears came true, it was nothing like I would have imagined back then. None of it was.

Non-verbal, non-sherbal. It might be the biggest fear for a parent like me, and I freely admit that it does take a toll sometimes. Things can be frustrating, but have you ever tried communicating with a verbal 16-year-old girl? I have. Nine times out of ten, it's easier to get a cohesive answer from my son's hand gestures than it is from his sister's overflowing vocabulary. Lack of language isn't the end of the world. It just takes our innate desire to connect to our children by any means necessary and puts it to the test.

Consider the movie *Poltergeist*, where parents lose their daughter to an interdimensional void and work tirelessly with an eccentric parade of experts to reconnect with her. This 80s horror film illustrates the depths parents go through to get through to their children. My kid uses an iPad to speak. Their kid was stuck in the freakin' wall. If they can do it, I can.

Just as the parents overcome supernatural barriers, nothing can prevent me from connecting with Lucas. Despite common misconceptions, my boy is very much present and engaged. He isn't just someone to be looked after; he's an active, integral member of our family. Over the years, we've worked hard to understand each other better and ensure he remains an included and cherished member of our family circle, regardless of the challenges.

It's not some big deal, although people may think so. The reason why they feel that way is because they imagine themselves in our situation. They envision all that Lucas needs me to do to help him get through his day and create situations they're not entirely sure about. Then they paint a blurry picture of themselves doing tireless work for a kid that they don't yet have.

I know this is true because that's what I did when he was a baby and it's why I feared autism. I saw only the heartache and work for a kid he hadn't yet become. I pictured doing the direst of tasks for an imaginary stranger. Who wouldn't think that seems hellacious?

If you're one of those people, let me straighten it out for you. Forget the imagined kid. Imagine your real kid, if you have one. What would you do if your neurotypical son or daughter had an accident and suddenly needed care for the rest of their lives? This isn't some new child you dreamed up. This is a real person you know right now. It's someone you already have and love. Would you shudder at the thought of being their caretaker and walk away?

No. You would do whatever you could to make them happy and help them thrive. You'd quit your job and save every penny you found to give them the best life you can. It's a no-brainer. That's what a parent does. So why does it surprise you that I do it for my child with a smile on my face? It's been his whole life. It's all we've ever known.

People do this every day. Actually, forget the kids; it applies easier to others in our lives. We do it for our parents and our loved ones. I have known people who put their lives on hold to care for their ailing moms or dads. They happily do what they can to make their lives easier and more comfortable, no matter how difficult it is on them personally. Your loved one needs you, so you do it. Is it easy? No. But you're family and that's what family does. You don't run. You're home team.

So, yes. Many of the worst-case-scenario things came true in our life, and they don't look as I expected. My boy is non-verbal, and with that comes the need for assistance, most likely for the rest of his life. He has challenges that I need to help him through. When I can't do it, I'll need to have someone in place who can. Lucas is a responsibility that will outlive me.

CHAPTER 24

Right Back to the Beginning

Rethinking What You Assume Fatherhood Would Be

Let's finish the book by going right back to the start. Lucas was born in March 2011. At the time, I was wearing a gray sweatshirt with three rather large buttons and a pair of dark jeans. It was my go-to outfit, the most comfortable combination in my closet, and one that I would be wearing again on another monumental day of my life, but that's a story we haven't gotten to yet.

Full disclosure—I find the whole process of baby-birthing to be stressful, and before you shout "It's more stressful for the woman," hear me out. That's where a lot of the stress came from.

The stress comes from worry about the things that could go wrong. In the days before my life changed, I spent a lot of time worrying about what-ifs. While that would eventually change in grand fashion, it was still the case when my son came along.

At the time, I was always concerned about something and the risk of childbirth was a big one. After all, back in *Little House on the Prairie* times, people were dying left and right while trying to pop out a baby. I get that the process is now safer with electricity, but it still felt like I could lose most of my family in one fell swoop.

My then-wife was carrying my unborn child. If something happens to her, something would happen to him. It would be like having an unbelievable tragedy play out on multiple levels. Sound dark? I know it does, but that's how my brain worked back then. I would craft scenarios that didn't happen just to hurt my own feelings. It was crazy.

I was so grateful when my boy popped out all covered in goo with his head shaped like a cartoon anvil. I loved him right away, even if he looked like an alien.

Three years earlier, I felt that same immediate bond with his sister. Although Olivia's entrance was a bit different. She was a performer from the start. Upon delivery, she was crying. The sounds of baby sobs filled the room as they took her to the corner of the room. Then suddenly, the crying stopped.

I was scared something was wrong. When I turned to look, she was laying there underneath that little newborn tanning bed they put them on. Her hand was tucked under her chin as she peered off into the distance. It was like she was posing for her closeup. The scene was adorable, and as the years have ticked by, I've learned that it was an early preview of her personality.

Lucas wasn't performing. All misshapen and gooey, he was a little lumpy fella. Just like his sister, he was cute. For some reason, though, it just felt like he would be more fragile. At the time, I chalked it up to seeing him as the baby of the family, but something inside me said that I needed to take care of this boy. I looked into his little face and felt a sense of protection.

Three days of my life changed me. These were two of them. Having kids drastically shifts your priorities without even having to make a concerted effort. It just happens naturally. From that day on, the food in my house has been purchased with them in mind. Gift cards I get for holidays are used to buy them the things they need. The jobs I take, the money I make, and the time I have are all for them. I don't even need to think about it. I just do it.

People seem to forget that dads are supposed to have that obligation baked into their souls too. They can see that point of view for moms, yet take pictures of men carrying unicorn backpacks for their daughters and post them online as if it's something so amazing. It's just another example of the bar being lowered to the ground for male parents. Who the hell is going to tell his little girl he won't hold her backpack because it's too girly? It makes no sense.

To me, parenthood always felt like the coolest job a person could ever have. You get to be the example of adulthood to someone and teach them everything you've learned in life. You're a guide who, at least in the early years, is treated like a celebrity. Although if you have a kid like Lucas you get treated that way all the time.

It's instinct. You don't even need to come from good parents to be a good parent. For those who were mistreated, abused, or abandoned, it doesn't have to define the parent you go on to be. For those who weren't shown how to love a son or daughter by the people tasked with raising you, there's an easy way to break that cycle. You can simply be the adult figure in their lives that you always wished for in your own.

That's what I did.

To me, that actually felt like the more admirable and rewarding starting point to come from. You get to be the superhero to someone else every day, and know, firsthand, the impact you're having. Those missing love and support in childhood recognize how important it is to give. They've experienced the pain of missing out and can now help their own children never experience such a feeling. To be denied love during a difficult time and then be able to give that love to someone else is amazing. You know you're putting good into the world.

Fathers play an important role in the lives of their kids, whether they are there or not. It feels obvious. We see it in the positive relationships that male father figures have with their children. Even more so, we see it reflected in those who didn't have those father figures and grew up with "daddy issues."

That's a term that needs no explanation. We all know the damage that can be done by a parent unwilling to be the strength that a child needs in life. Yet so many seem to forget this commonsense thing when growing up and switching roles.

We're a generation of adults crying at home about how our parents missed our Little League games while our kids are off playing Little League alone. That's true. Put it in a fortune cookie and crack it open. Give it to someone you love.

Phrases like "absentee fathers" ring out from armchair psychologists as if they're unavoidable natural disasters plaguing our youth. It's like leaving a rabid dog on your front porch and wondering why all your visitors are bleeding when they show up. If only something could be done.

With everyone recognizing the need for positive male figures in the lives of our children, I assumed the world would welcome a devoted dad with open arms. Seeing how involved I wanted to be, those who complain about missing men within a family would surely acknowledge my place.

Yeah. Not really.

Before my first child was even born, and long before my phone call with the porcupine-sitting Fairy Godmother, I got my first view of this backward mentality.

I was at a dinner party with my then-wife's not-so-likable friends. Expectedly, they had even less likable friends who had joined us that night. Having never met these people prior to that evening, I could tell almost immediately that they enjoyed attention.

HI WORLD, I'M DAD

The tales they told were loud and opinionated. These were the type of folks who spoke about strangers you never met as if you knew them. We'd hear anecdotes about "Jerry and Martha," with no clue who the hell Jerry and Martha were. It was that sort of slow-drip pain over a serving of brisket that we all suffer through in our twenties. Lord help me.

In one of the most memorable moments from that evening, this couple began talking about their baby. It was then that the wife decided to share this shocking story of exclusion in her bougie Brooklyn community.

"Martin was home from work last week on a Tuesday. So we took Baby Madison to the card store to get a card for Simon's birthday. He was pushing the cart down one of the aisles and a woman refused to move. Huh! Can you believe that? Refused! I was shocked. We figured out why, though. It was a Tuesday. She must have thought Martin was a stay-at-home dad. Isn't that ridiculous?"

Sounds like a positive. This woman was standing up for the men of the world against the judgmental eyes of another. Noble, right? Not quite. Just wait. There's more.

"It's like, 'No, lady. He works. He just took the day off. He's not some stay-at-home dad.' Could you imagine? How dare she think that? The nerve of some people!"

Everyone laughed. Through the laughter, one guest meekly asked, "Even so, what if he was? What's wrong with a stay-at-home dad?"

No one responded to that. The conversation shifted to Jerry's Lasik surgery.

Even without any children yet, I knew this thinking was warped. It felt like someone remarking how terrible it would be for a female to become a mechanic. What year is it? The undefined disdain for a man potentially doing the thing that everyone says they want men to do more made no sense. It was my first introduction to the hypocrisy that I would eventually encounter as a father.

Regardless, I haven't let it change me or the way I parent my children. My goal has always been to be an involved dad. I didn't play with dolls or pretend to be a daddy at recess, but that didn't make a difference. My reason for wanting to be active in the lives of my children wasn't because it reminded me of my toys growing up; it was because I knew I'd love my children and wanted to show them the best parts of life.

As a side note, that's a bizarre way to view a parent's motivations. If we all spent adulthood emulating the toys we grew up playing with, there would be a lot more dads harnessing the power of Castle Grayskull and working as Power Rangers. I mean, come on. What world do these people live in?

If you want to talk about gender, there's a classic "manly" reason for staying active in your kids' lives. Sure, there's the sense of responsibility and all that stuff, but what about the fact that I'm sending tiny little representations of myself into the world every day? How can you not work to make sure you're teaching them to be the best people around? In the very least, it's Public Relations 101. If your kid's a jerk, that blows back on you. This is your family legacy we're talking about here.

Still not enough? Okay. Aside from sculpting their personalities and being responsible for them, what about simply loving them? That's a pretty big reason to stay active, right? If you can't love people you actually made yourself, then how can you love anyone else? I'm sorry if I sound glib, but I genuinely have never been able to understand how any parent can walk away from his or her children, especially when they're young. You brought them here.

Make no mistake. Walking away doesn't just mean physically. For every dad that went to get milk and never came back, there are ten who remained in the house and became part of the furniture. Ironically, that feels almost worse because the lack of care is right there on display for everyone to notice.

This holds true for any gender. Moms could emotionally or physically leave too. At the end of the day, your child is your responsibility. Male, female, or any way you identify doesn't change the fact that the possibility of disinterested parenting could exist.

None of those things is the sole reason I am here for my children. I'm here because something inside me just makes me. It's just part of who I am and the core of my being. I feel a connection to my kids and I feel like a superhero to them every day.

In turn, they put me on a higher pedestal than the rest of the world. Even when they might not show it, I know that I am one of the two most important people they'll ever know. Our kids talk about us long after we're gone. They tell the world who we are and keep our spirits alive. Who wouldn't want to nurture a relationship like that?

Adding in my son's special needs and lack of language doesn't change that sense of obligation. If anything, I know my boy needs me. Just like that first day when his alien spaceship touched down in the hospital, I felt the need to protect him. He may not tell people about me, but the man he becomes will be a reflection on the way I raised him.

For many fathers, there is a laundry list of reasons behind why they struggle to maintain their responsibilities for the person they brought into the world. Typically, it's about past trauma, current heartache, and a lack of role models in their personal lives.

While I don't discount anyone else's struggle, I can tell you that I experienced all three of those things in my own life. I wasn't shown the proper way to raise children at a young age, and there are no family members from my youth around to help with my parenting today.

None of us like to detail painful and scary memories. I include myself in that, so I won't do it here. I will tell you, however, that if I wanted to hang my hat on those issues as a reason to avoid parenting correctly today, I could. Others would give me a pass, a pat on the head, and a sad story at my funeral, if I allowed it.

HI WORLD, I'M DAD

But I don't. I don't because I'm a father. I owe these kids the best life they could have, and even on my hardest days, I suck it up and push forward. Negative voices will always swirl around in my head. My goal is to make sure they don't swirl around in the heads of my kids one day. Being involved today is how I ensure that doesn't happen.

I owe them that much.

Conclusion

I don't see my son as simply disabled. While he has specialized needs, he also has so much more. He's the most honest, pure, and unfiltered person I've ever had the pleasure to know. That's why we appreciate him.

Why do you love your own children? Ask anyone and they will give you a bookshelf's worth of stories about how cute their kids either are or used to be. Some of the stories aren't even good. Yet to hear the parent tell it, it's the greatest anecdote since Aesop. They talk about their little ones with beaming pride.

Do you know who else does that? Special needs parents do that. If you have one in your life and they feel comfortable with you, you'll hear humorous tales about their child's daily activities. Many of us, in fact, are desperate to tell people. It's hard to share stories about my son for fear I will be stopped short with a sympathetic face or words of pity. I hate it, and I would rather keep my tales private than have someone look down on my son.

But when I trust someone and feel safe that they see my boy for the wonder that he is, I am more than willing to talk about Lucas all day. It's why I stand so firmly behind the idea of autism appreciation. Simply put, I'm not the only one who sees what we should appreciate. There are many other parents like me who do too.

Parents with children like my son know the unique ways in which their kids see the world. They have funny tales that others might not fully comprehend. That's only because they weren't there and can't understand the context. This is who my son is. This is why I love him. Other people don't live here, so you might not get it.

What's funny to us seems tragic to others because they're so fixated on the idea of wishing he could talk or be different. I've accepted that fact, and his humorous tales, even the ones that sound difficult or fraught with his inability to understand, draw a smile from those who know us.

And that's why I write about him. Lucas has a million stories every day that I can retell to give you a glimpse into a rare gem in this world. The things he does and the ways in which he carries himself are so profoundly Lucas that you need to see it firsthand.

Typing them out and posting them allows me to share these tales without having to endure a sad face from a listener or a reaction that makes me regret telling them. I get to hold on to the happiness the story brings me without allowing someone else's misguided fear push me away from it.

I'm not even talking about good stories of triumph either. I'm talking about times like when I brought my then-four-year-old boy to the local school playground with a container of giant chalk. I had convinced myself that he was going to be an artist, I was going to teach Lucas to draw a masterpiece, and one day he would thank me on stage for his chalk artist Academy Award.

So we rolled over to the empty schoolyard in his little red wagon and I began drawing on the blacktop while he ran all over like a speed demon. Finally, I walked over and led him back by the hand to show him what I was doing. He knelt down beside me on the blacktop.

"Look. Lucas, look. Chalk. You draw."

And that's what I did. I held this oversized pink chalk stick in my hand and made a line on the ground. For some reason, I repeated "Chaallllk" as I did. Then I turned to my little preschooler.

"You do. Chalk."

We locked eyes. He looked down at the chalk and back at me. I felt like I was in the Helen Keller movie. I was ready to accept my greatest-dad ever award. Here comes the art. The magic was about to happen.

He looked at me again and then back at my hand. Slowly, he

reached over and barely fit his tiny little fist around this gigantic piece of chalk. Then he looked up at me.

And shoved the entire thing into his mouth.

Like the baby-pillow-music incident, it took a few seconds to register what was happening before I hurriedly fished it out of his face and saved his life…again…for the tenth time that day.

Hopefully you laughed at that, because I did. It's completely true too. Those who don't understand what it's like to have accepted their child's challenges will hang their heads and pity me for having a child who doesn't understand the importance of chalk. Everyone else will laugh and say, "That's so Lucas!" Those with kids like him in their own life will usually share a story that mirrors it.

It's funny. It was funny when it happened and endearing. If my son was able to understand stories in the traditional sense, I guarantee he would laugh too. You can't laugh at the things you fear. That's how we're able to smile in the face of crossed signals and lost translations.

Autism doesn't end your world; it just opens the door to one you never knew existed. As for the challenges, they can be tough, but they're worth the trade-off and are completely manageable. In fact, they are routine in our lives and just another part of my day. They may be work-intensive and pretty important parts of my day, but routine just the same.

Why don't these challenges feel as daunting in practice

as they sound on paper? Because we've adapted. Lucas is worth every effort. He's not just a set of needs. He's a person who brings immense joy and uniqueness to our lives. His challenges don't define him. I do things for him, just as I would for his sister. I owe them and love them. Helping them isn't a burden. It's my obligation and my pleasure.

Life is inherently tough, but no challenge, be it a lack of speech or a cinematic supernatural poltergeist event, could ever stop me from supporting Lucas. In our family, every obstacle is an opportunity to demonstrate our love and commitment. We work together and overcome anything.

There were tons of worries at first. I tried to predict what was to come. In the end, nothing looked the way I envisioned, and the positive parts were never even part of the early equations of fear. When you're living in a time period spent listening to warnings about things that could cause "delays" for your child, there is little in the way of positive things to picture.

Well, I come from the future and I've seen the life I dreaded a decade ago. It all came true. Every terrible outcome came to pass, and all the scary things I told myself would be the end of the world, if they happened, happened. This is the exact situation I worried about and tried to see through my fuzzy imagination.

And it's perfect. He's perfect. We're perfect. Life is as it should be and we couldn't be happier.

Lucas's "worst-case-scenario" was anything but worst. He

lives his life at the maximum volume and feels things brighter than any color you could imagine. The joy that exudes from this kid lights up any room he's in, and he doesn't need anything except for love, patience, and acceptance.

My son is non-verbal and he has autism. It's a sentence that would have left me destroyed a decade ago. Today, it's part of our lives and one of the things I appreciate most about him. I'm thankful that the universe brought him into our family, presented the opportunity to know the most unique individual I've ever met, and showed me the love he brings to our lives.

Is he tough to care for? You bet. All kids are. Is he worth it? Like you wouldn't believe.

Autism isn't the end of the world; it's a whole different one with beauty you never knew existed. I love my non-verbal son. If you knew him, you would too.

There's nothing wrong with my son. He's real and he's perfect. Autism makes him that way. That's the other thing I know for sure.